Ukulele Songs FOR DUMMIES®

Performance Notes by Chad Johnson

ISBN 978-1-4234-9604-5

HAL•LEONARD®
CORPORATION

7777 W. BLUEMOUND RD. P.O. BOX 13819 MILWAUKEE, WI 53213

Visit Hal Leonard Online at
www.halleonard.com

Table of Contents

Introduction

Welcome to *Ukulele Songs For Dummies*. In this book, you'll find 50 classic songs to play on ukulele — from classic rock and pop gems like "Brown Eyed Girl" to modern hits like "Hey, Soul Sister" to musical classics like "Supercalifragilisticexpialidocious." Notes are included for each song that help with any technical challenges and provide you with a bit of song history for the trivia buffs out there.

Although this book is a helpful instructional tool, the material contained within is most likely too difficult for a beginner. If you're brand new to the instrument, you should probably pick up a book for beginners, such as *Ukulele For Dummies* by Alistair Wood (Wiley), before tackling the songs in this book.

About This Book

For each song in the book, you'll get some fun background information followed by the essentials needed to play the song:

- Chord grids for every chord used
- The vocal melody for those wanting some melodic practice
- Harmonic information on the chord progressions
- Explanations of any specific chart symbols or directions (such as repeat signs, D.S. indications, and so on)

If you're already familiar with this information, feel free to skip ahead and start strumming (or plucking). If you enjoy playing melodies on the uke, it's recommended that you work through the chords first before tackling the melody, as this will familiarize you with the basic framework of the song. If melodic playing isn't your thing, just strum through the songs and croon (if you're so inclined)!

How to Use This Book

The songs in this book are presented in a modified lead sheet format. A *lead sheet* is a form of notation that allows you to play the accompaniment or melody of a song with which you're not familiar. It normally features the vocal melody (assuming it's a vocal song) and chord symbols and may contain any significant melodic contributions from other instruments. In this book, chord grids have been added beneath every chord symbol that show you exactly how to play them on the ukulele. There are many different ways to play the same chord on the ukulele, and if you're familiar with other ways (or *chord voicings*, as they're known), feel free to substitute them. At any rate, the chord grids shown in this book are a great place to start.

At the end of the book, there's a chart of common chords and scales for the uke. You'll no doubt see many of these chords in the songs presented. It might be a good idea to play through them first thing to see if there are any that are new to you. The scales will help you become familiar with individual notes on the instrument should you choose to try playing a vocal melody.

There's also a page on basic chord harmony at the end. This will help make sense of the harmonic discussion that appears in the songs and provide you with invaluable information that will aid in your musical growth. By understanding how basic chord progressions work, you'll be able to more easily communicate with other musicians, and you'll be armed with the foundation needed to start writing your own songs if you choose.

Conventions used in this book

Here are some common musical terms you'll see throughout the discussions in this book:

- **Chord progressions:** The sequence of chords used in a song.
- **Barre chords:** Chords that require you to "barre," or lay flat, a finger across several strings at the same fret.
- **Open chords**: Chords that include an open string and don't require a barre.
- **Open strings:** Strings played open — without a finger fretting them.
- **Strumming:** The act of playing through all four strings with one brisk stroke — either down toward the floor, as in a *downstroke*, or up toward the ceiling, as in an *upstroke*.
- **Scales:** A collection of notes, usually seven different notes, from which the melody of a song is derived; the most common scales are the major scale and minor scale.

What about lefties?

Left-handed players often get the shaft when trying to locate instruments, and that sadly transfers into written materials as well. So if you find any instances of the picking hand being referred to as the right hand or the fretting hand referred to as the left hand, please don't take it personally! Just flip the directions, and you'll be good to go.

Melodies on the uke

The ukulele, along with the five-string banjo, is unique in the fact that the strings don't progress uniformly from low to high in pitch like a guitar or violin. The strings on the uke are typically tuned, from fourth to first: G–C–E–A. But the G note is higher in pitch than the C and E strings (it's just lower in pitch than the A string). Although this is part of the uke's allure with regards to the sound of strumming chords, it makes for awkward melody playing on the G string. Therefore, most players stick to the third, second, and first strings when playing melodies.

Icons Used in This Book

In the margins of this book you'll find lots of little icons designed to make your life easier:

Useful details that you need to know. They'll probably show up in other songs tagged here.

This is where you'll find notes about specific musical terms or concepts that are relevant but can be confusing to the layperson.

These are suggestions and/or shortcuts that can help make things easier in general.

All You Need Is Love

Words and Music by John Lennon and Paul McCartney

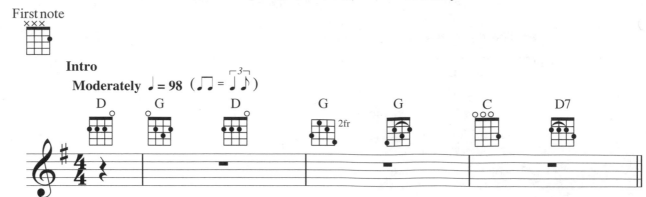

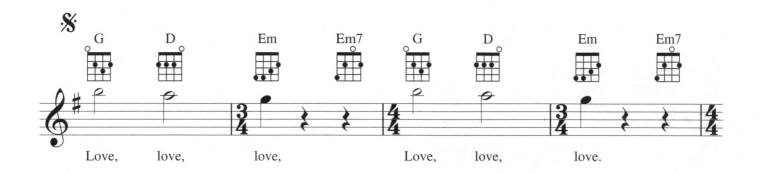

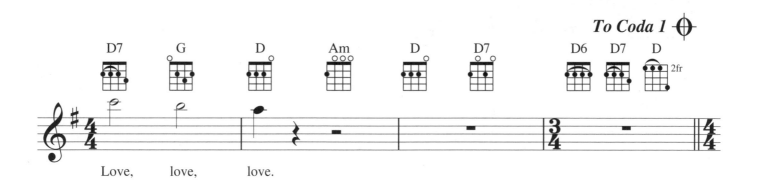

Noth - ing you can sing ___ that can't be sung. ___
No one you can save ___ that can't ___ be saved. ___
Noth - ing you can see ___ that is - n't shown. ___

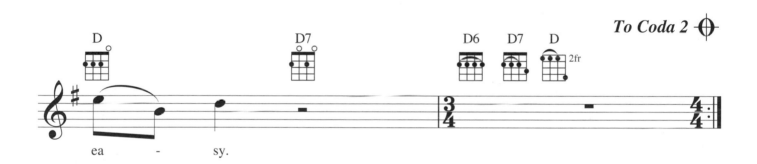

Noth - ing you can say, but you can learn how to play the game.
No - thing you can do, but you can learn ___ how to be you in time. } It's
There's no - where you can be that is - n't where ___ you're meant to be. ___ }

To Coda 2

ea - sy.

Chorus

All you need is love. ___

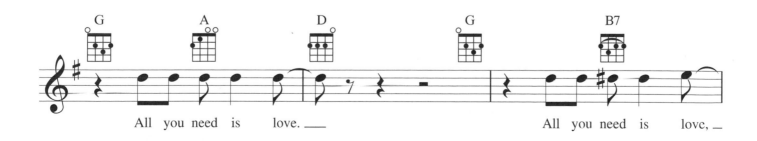

All you need is love. ___   All you need is love, ___

D.S. al Coda 1

— love. —   Love is all — you need. —

⊕ Coda 1

All   you   need   is   love. ____

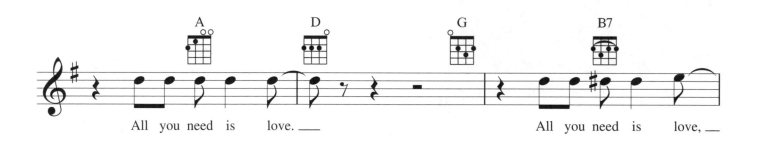

All you need is   love. ____   All you need is   love, —

D.S.S. al Coda 2
(no repeat)

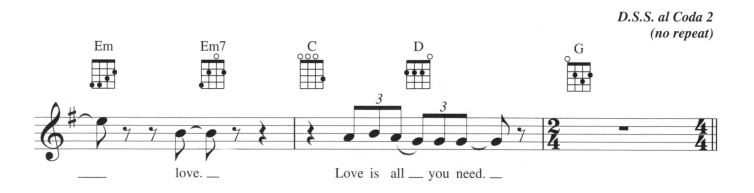

— love. —   Love is all — you need. —

⊕ Coda 2
Chorus

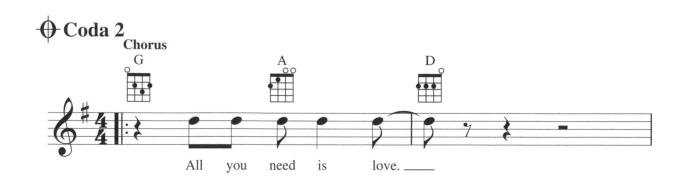

All   you   need   is   love. ____

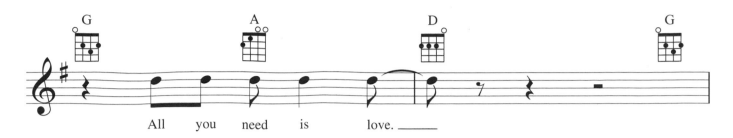

All you need is love. _____

All you need is love, _____ love. ___

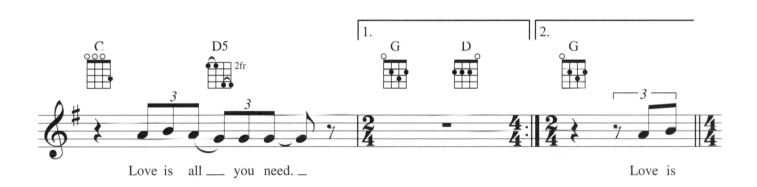

Love is all ___ you need. ___ Love is

Outro

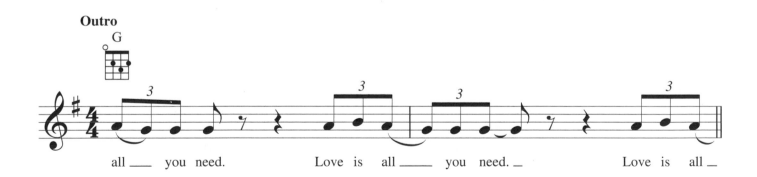

all ___ you need. Love is all _____ you need. _ Love is all _

Play 12 times and fade

___ you need. _ Love is all _____ you need. _ Love is all __

Bali Ha'i

from SOUTH PACIFIC
Lyrics by Oscar Hammerstein II
Music by Richard Rodgers

(It's A) Beautiful Morning

Words and Music by Felix Cavaliere and Edward Brigati, Jr.

It's your chance to wake up and plan ___ an - oth - er
It just ain't no good if the sun ___ shines and you're

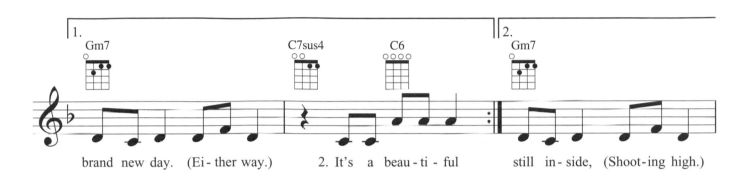

1.
brand new day. (Ei - ther way.) 2. It's a beau - ti - ful

2.
still in - side, (Shoot-ing high.)

Still in - side, (Shoot-ing high.) ___ Still in - side. (Shoot-ing high.) Oh, oh. _____

Interlude

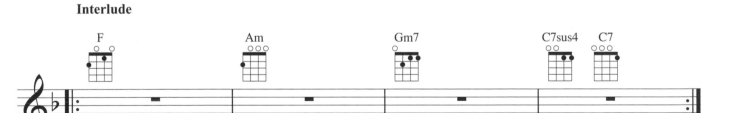

Bridge

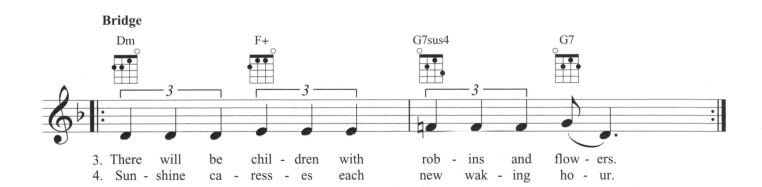

3. There will be chil - dren with rob - ins and flow - ers.
4. Sun - shine ca - ress - es each new wak - ing ho - ur.

Seems to me ___ that peo-ple keep see - ing more and more to-day. (Got - ta say.)

Lead the way. (It's o - kay.) _ Brand new day. (Got - ta say.) It's o - kay. (All the way.)

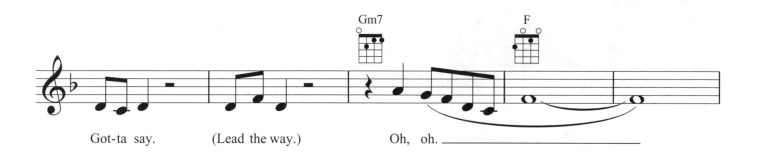

Got-ta say. (Lead the way.) Oh, oh. _____

Outro

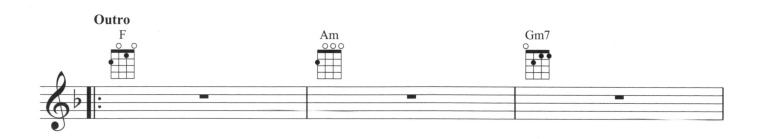

Oh, oh. _____

Brown Eyed Girl

Words and Music by Van Morrison

First note

Intro

Moderately fast Rock ♩ = 138

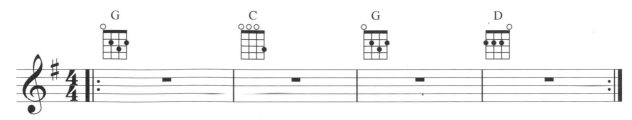

Verse

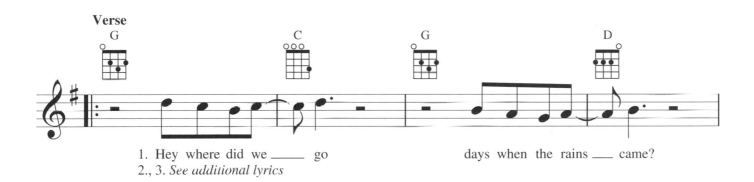

1. Hey where did we ___ go   days when the rains ___ came?
2., 3. *See additional lyrics*

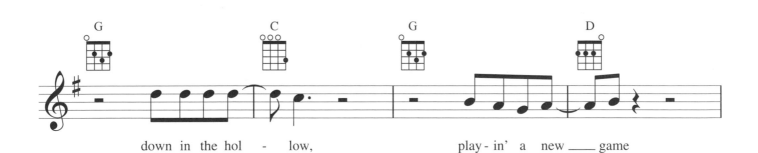

down in the hol - low,   play - in' a new ___ game

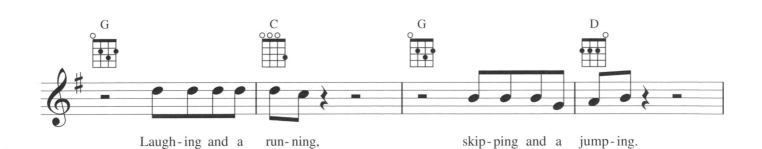

Laugh - ing and a   run - ning,   skip - ping and a   jump - ing.

in the mis - ty mor - ing fog ___ with our

hearts a thump - in', And you, _____ my brown eyed girl. __

___

You, _____ my brown eyed girl. ___

Do you re - mem - ber when __ we used to sing? __

Bridge

___ Sha, la, ___ la, la, ___ la, la, ___ la, la, ___ la, la, la, te, da. ___

Sha, la, ___ la, la, ___ la, la, ___ la, la, ___ la, la, la, te, da. ___

⊕ Coda

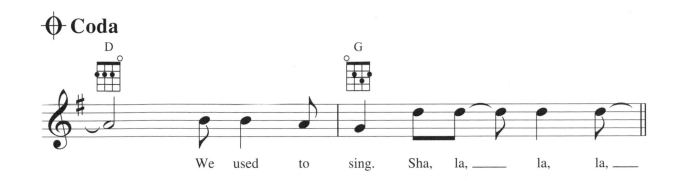

We used to sing. Sha, la, ___ la, la, ___

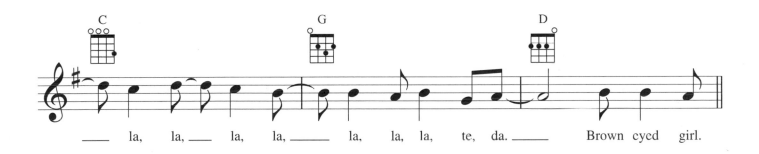

___ la, la, ___ la, la, ___ la, la, la, te, da. ___ Brown eyed girl.

Outro

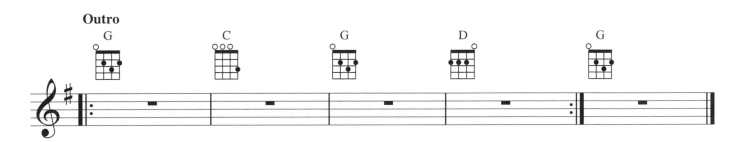

Additional Lyrics

2. Whatever happened
   To Tuesday and so slow?
   Going down the old mine.
   With a transistor radio.
   Standing in the sunlight laughing,
   Hiding behind a rainbow's wall ,
   Slipping and sliding
   All along the waterfall with you,
   My brown eyed girl.
   You, my brown eyed girl.

3. So hard to find my way
   Now that I'm all on my own.
   I saw you just the other day;
   My, how you have grown.
   Cast my mem'ry back there, Lord.
   Sometimes I'm overcome thinking 'bout it.
   Laughing and a running, hey, hey.
   Behind the stadium with you.
   My brown eyed girl.
   A you, my brown eyed girl.

Bibbidi-Bobbidi-Boo

(The Magic Song)

From Walt Disney's CINDERELLA
Words by Jerry Livingston
Music by Mack David and Al Hoffman

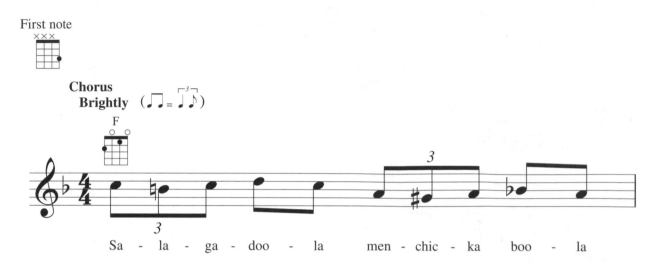

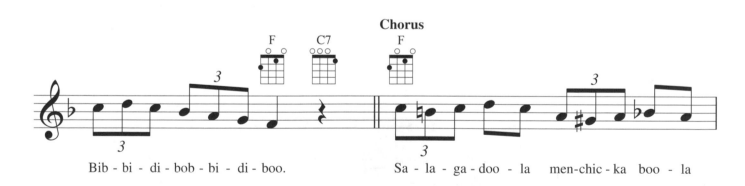

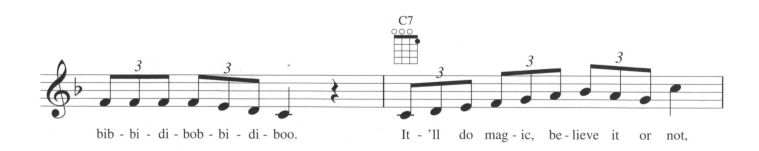

Verse

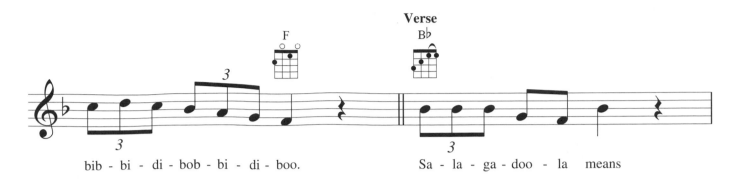

bib - bi - di - bob - bi - di - boo.　　　Sa - la - ga - doo - la　means

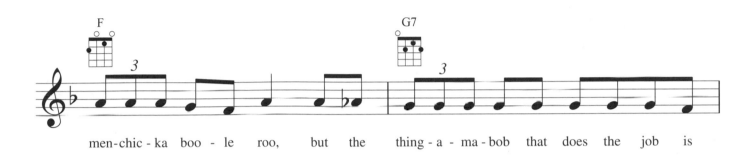

men - chic - ka　boo - le　roo,　but　the　thing - a - ma - bob　that　does　the　job　is

Chorus

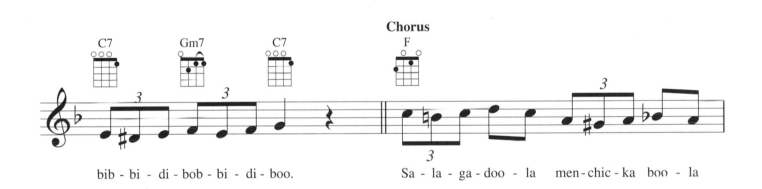

bib - bi - di - bob - bi - di - boo.　　　Sa - la - ga - doo - la　men - chic - ka　boo - la

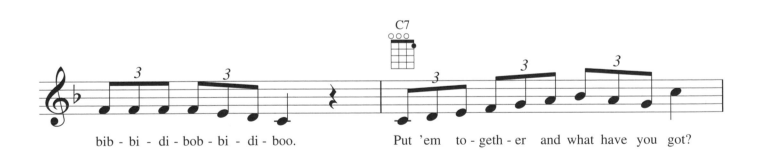

bib - bi - di - bob - bi - di - boo.　　　Put 'em　to - geth - er　and what have you got?

Bib - bi - di - bob - bi - di, bib - bi - di - bob - bi - di,　bib - bi - di - bob - bi - di - boo.

Blue Hawaii

from the Paramount Picture WAIKIKI WEDDING
Words and Music by Leo Robin and Ralph Rainger

First note

Verse
Slowly

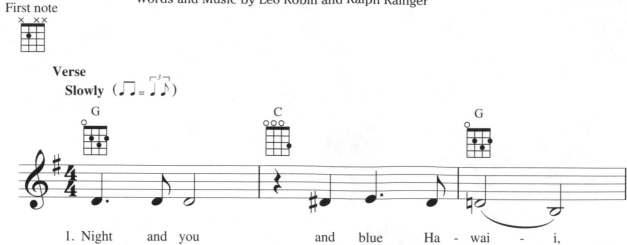

1. Night and you and blue Ha - wai - i,

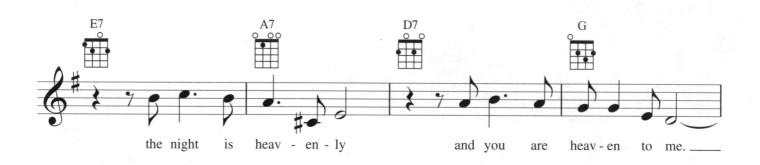

the night is heav - en - ly and you are heav - en to me. _____

Verse

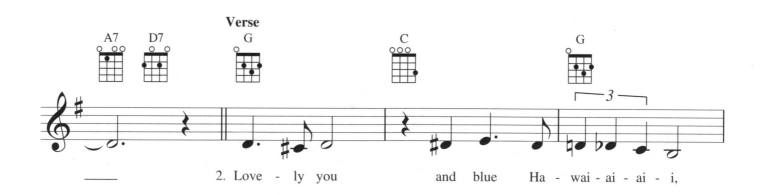

_____ 2. Love - ly you and blue Ha - wai - ai - ai - i,

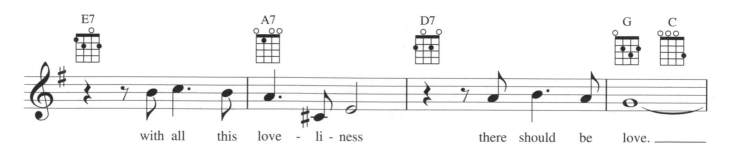

with all this love - li - ness there should be love. _____

Bye Bye Blackbird

from PETE KELLY'S BLUES
Lyric by Mort Dixon
Music by Ray Henderson

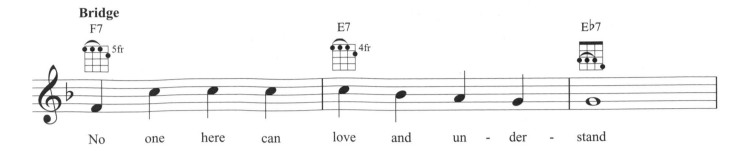

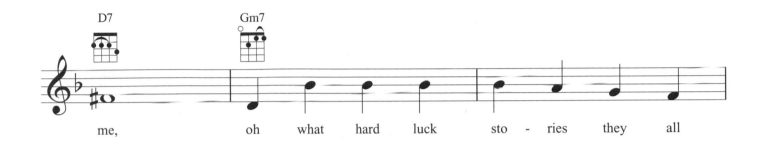

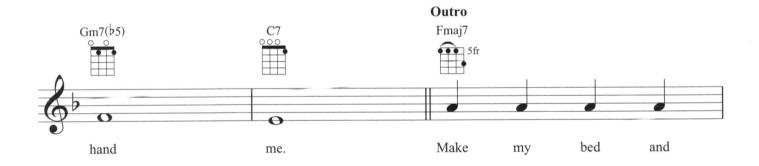

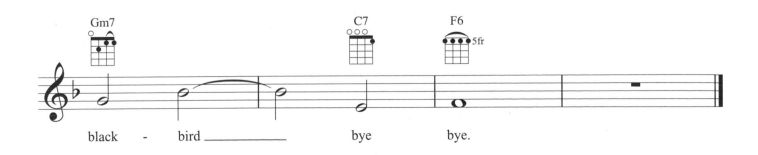

Can't Help Falling in Love

Words and Music by George David Weiss, Hugo Peretti and Luigi Creatore

Coconut

Words and Music by Harry Nilsson

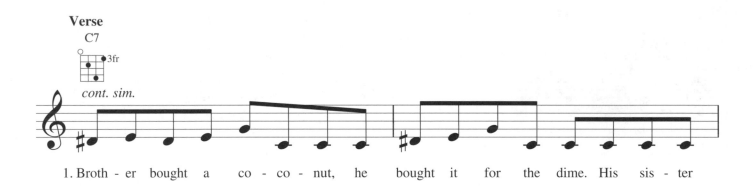

1. Broth-er bought a co-co-nut, he bought it for the dime. His sis-ter

had an-oth-er one, she paid it for the lime. ___ She put the

lime in the co-co-nut, she drank 'em both ___ up. She put the
lime in the co-co-nut, you drank 'em both ___ up, put the

lime   in   the   co - co - nut,   she   drank 'em   both ___ up.   She   put   the
lime   in   the   co - co - nut,   you   drank 'em   both   up,   put   the

lime   in   the   co - co - nut,   she   drank 'em   both ___ up.   She   put   the
lime   in   the   co - co - nut,   you   drank 'em   both ___ up,   put   the

lime   in   the   co - co - nut,   she   called the   doc - tor,   woke him up   and said,)
lime   in   the   co - co - nut,   you   called your   doc - tor,   woke him up   and said,)

Refrain

"Doc - tor,   ain't there   noth - in'   I   can   take,   I   said,   Doc -

- tor,   to   re - lieve   this   bel - ly   ache?   I   said,

To Coda 1 ⊕

Doc - tor,   ain't there   noth - in'   I   can   take,   I   said,

Doc - tor, to re - lieve this bel - ly ache?" Now

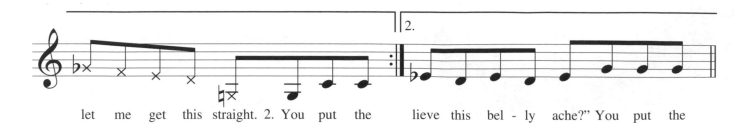

let me get this straight. 2. You put the lieve this bel - ly ache?" You put the

Chorus

C7

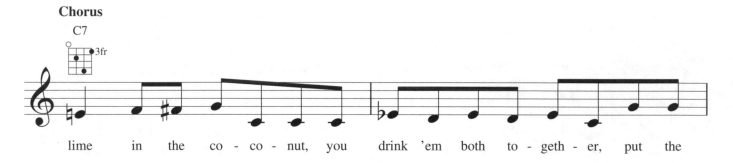

lime in the co - co - nut, you drink 'em both to - geth - er, put the

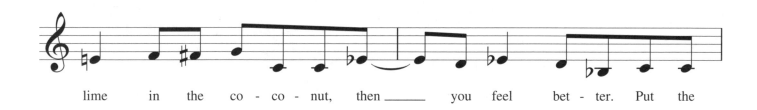

lime in the co - co - nut, then _____ you feel bet - ter. Put the

lime in the co - co - nut, drink 'em both ___ up, put the

lime in the co - co - nut and call me in the morn - ing.

Bridge

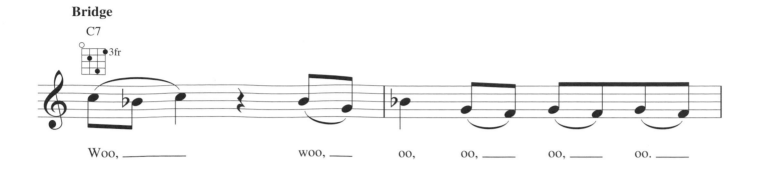

Woo, _____ woo, ___ oo, oo, _____ oo, _____ oo. _____

Oo, _____ woo, ___ oo, oo, oo, oo, _____ oo. _____

Oo, _____ oo, _____ oo, _____ oo, _____ oo, _____

___ oo, _____ oo, _____ oo, _____ oo, _____ oo. _____

Verse

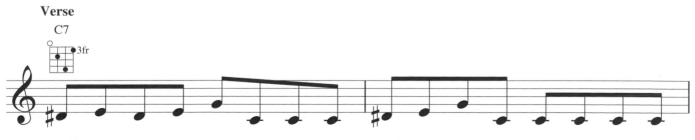

3. Broth - er bought a co - co - nut, he bought it for the dime. His sis - ter

D.S. al Coda 1
(take 1st lyrics)

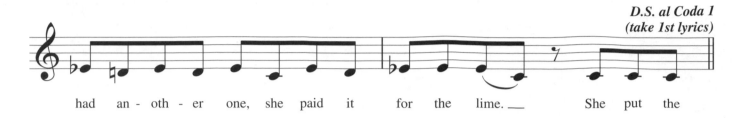

had   an - oth - er   one,   she   paid   it   for   the   lime. ___   She   put   the

Coda 1

Doc - tor,   now   let   me   get   this   straight."   4. You   put   the

𝄋:𝄋 Chorus

C7

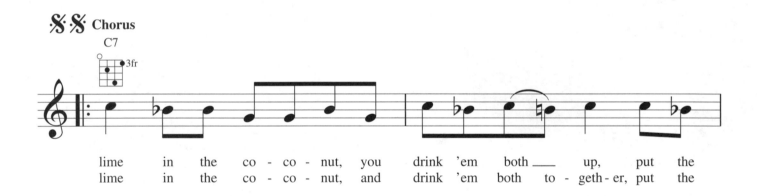

lime   in   the   co - co - nut,   you   drink 'em   both ___   up,   put   the
lime   in   the   co - co - nut,   and   drink 'em   both   to - geth - er,   put   the

lime   in   the   co - co - nut,   you   drink 'em   both ___   up,   the
lime   in   the   co - co - nut,   then   you   feel   bet - ter.   Put   the

To Coda 2

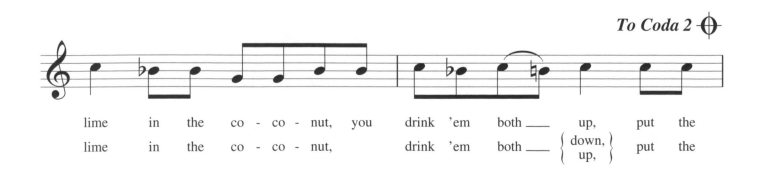

lime   in   the   co - co - nut,   you   drink 'em   both ___   up,   put   the
lime   in   the   co - co - nut,   drink 'em   both ___ { down, up, }   put   the

lime   in   the   co - co - nut, you're   such   a   sil - ly   wom - an.   Put   a
lime   in   the   co - co - nut,   and

Refrain

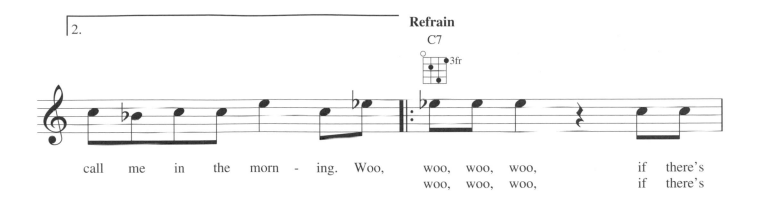

call   me   in   the   morn - ing.   Woo,   woo,   woo,   woo,   if   there's
woo,   woo,   woo,   if   there's

noth - ing   you   can   take,   I   said,   woo,   woo,   woo,   woo,   to   re -
noth - ing   I   can   take."   I   say,   woo, _____   woo,   to   re -

lieve   your   bel - ly   ache. You   say, "Well,   lieve   your   bel - ly   ache. You   say, "Yeah, ___

_____   if   there's   noth - ing   I   can   take."   I   say,   wow, _
_____   da,   if   there's   noth - ing   I   can   take.   I   say,   dat, _
_____   da,   if   there's   noth - ing   I   can   take.   I   say,   dat, _

1., 2.
—— wow, to re - lieve this bel - ly ache. I say, dat, _
—— da, if there's noth - ing I can take, I say dat, _

3.

D.S.S. al Coda 2
(take 2nd lyrics)

—— da. You're such a sil - ly wom - an. Put the

Coda 2

lime ———— in the co - co - nut and

Outro

C7

3fr

call me in the morn - ing. Yes, you call __

—— me in the morn - ing, when you call me in the morn - ing, I'll tell __

Repeat and fade

—— you what to do. If you call me in the morn - ing, I'll tell ——

'Deed I Do

Words and Music by Walter Hirsch and Fred Rose

1. Do I _____ want you? _____ Oh my, _____ do I? _____ Hon - ey, _____ 'deed I do!
2. Do I _____ need you? _____ Oh my, _____ do I? _____ Hon - ey, _____ 'deed I
3. Do I _____ love you? _____ Oh my, _____ do I? _____ Hon - ey, _____ 'deed I

do! _____ I'm glad that I'm the one who found you, that's why I'm al - ways hang - in' 'round you. do!

Dream a Little Dream of Me

Words by Gus Kahn
Music by Wilbur Schwandt and Fabian Andree

Easter Parade

featured in the Motion Picture Irving Berlin's EASTER PARADE
Words and Music by Irving Berlin

Edelweiss

from the SOUND OF MUSIC
Lyrics by Oscar Hammerstein II
Music by Richard Rodgers

Bridge

Blos - som of snow, may you bloom and

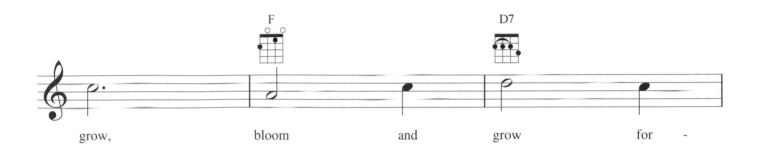

grow, bloom and grow for -

Chorus

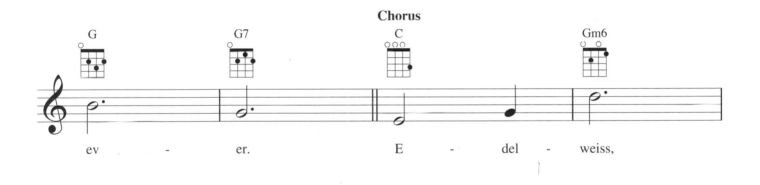

ev - er. E - del - weiss,

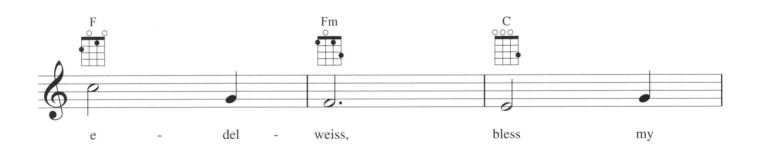

e - del - weiss, bless my

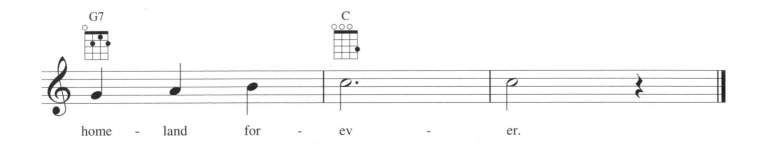

home - land for - ev - er.

Eleanor Rigby

Words and Music by John Lennon and Paul McCartney

First note

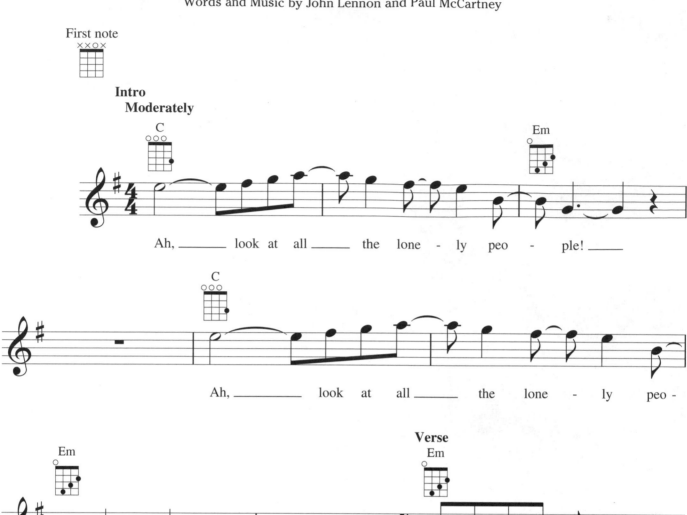

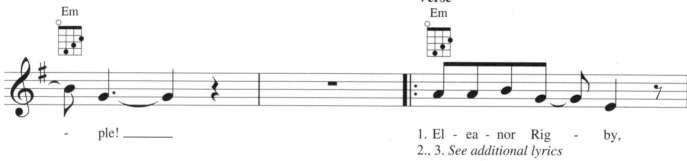

Additional Lyrics

2. Father McKenzie writing the words of a sermon that no one will hear,
No one comes near.
Look at him working, darning his socks in the night when there's nobody there,
What does he care?

3. Eleanor Rigby died in the church and was buried along with her name,
Nobody came.
Father McKenzie, wiping the dirt from his hands as he walks from the grave,
No one was saved.

Five Foot Two, Eyes of Blue
(Has Anybody Seen My Girl?)

Words by Joe Young and Sam Lewis
Music by Ray Henderson

The Fool on the Hill

Words and Music by John Lennon and Paul McCartney

First note

1. Day af-ter day, a-lone on a hill, ____ the
2. Well on the way, head in a cloud, ____ the

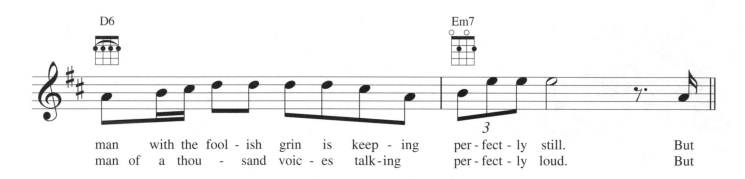

man with the fool-ish grin is keep-ing per-fect-ly still. But
man of a thou - sand voic-es talk-ing per-fect-ly loud. But

Pre-Chorus

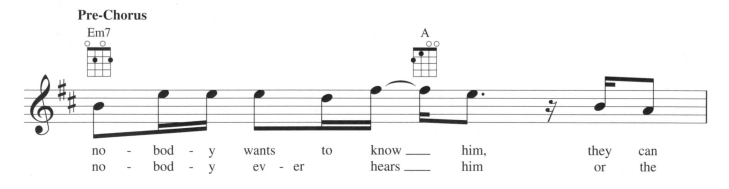

no - bod - y wants to know ____ him, they can
no - bod - y ev - er hears ____ him or the

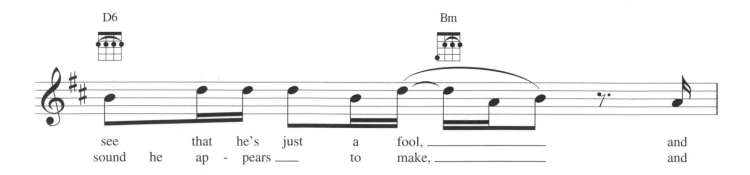

see that he's just a fool, ____ and
sound he ap - pears ____ to make, ____ and

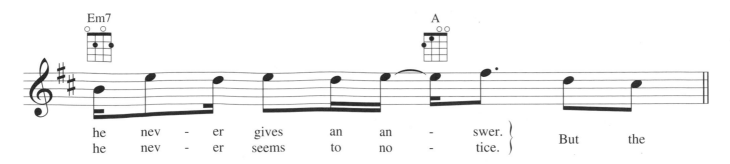

he nev - er gives an an - swer. But the
he nev - er seems to no - tice.

Chorus

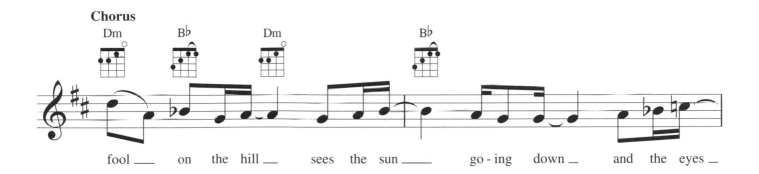

fool ___ on the hill ___ sees the sun ___ go - ing down ___ and the eyes ___

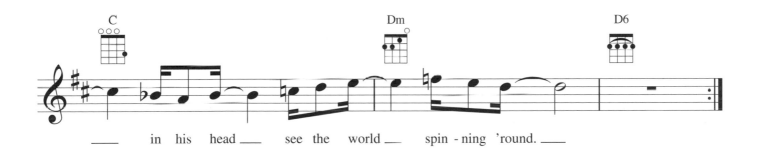

___ in his head ___ see the world ___ spin - ning 'round. ___

Recorder Solo

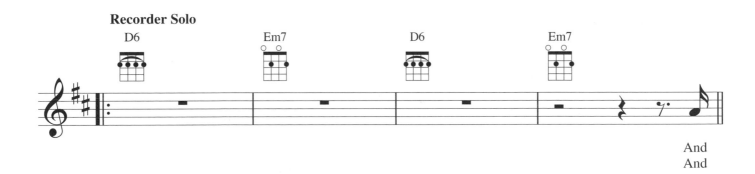

And
And

Pre-Chorus

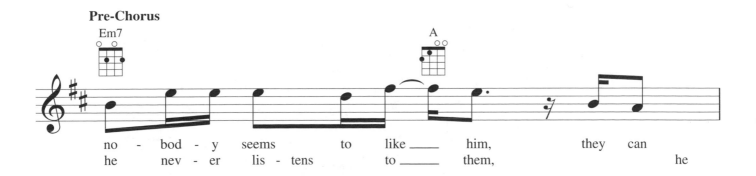

no - bod - y seems to like ___ him, they can
he nev - er lis - tens to ___ them, he

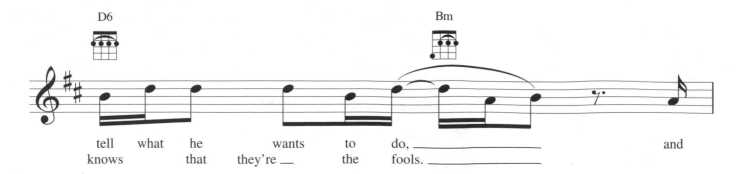

tell   what   he   wants   to   do, _____   and
knows   that   they're __   the   fools. _____

he   nev - er   shows   his   feel - ings.   But   the   fool __
They   don't   like _____   him.   The   fool __

Chorus

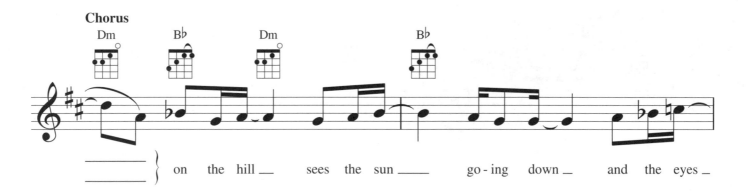

_____ }   on   the   hill __   sees   the   sun _____   go - ing   down __   and   the   eyes __

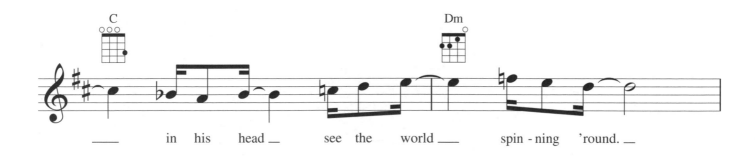

___   in   his   head __   see   the   world ___   spin - ning   'round. __

Outro   *Repeat and fade*

Oh, _____   a - round 'n' 'round 'n' 'round 'n' 'round.

The Gambler

Words and Music by Don Schlitz

First note

Verse
Moderate Country Two-step ♩ = 92

1. On a warm sum-mer's eve-nin' on a train bound for no-

-where, __ I met up with the gam - bler, we were

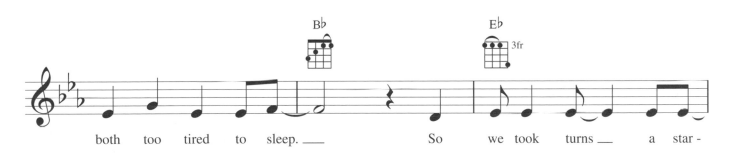

both too tired to sleep. __ So we took turns __ a star-

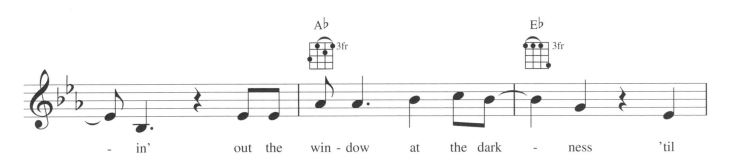

-in' out the win-dow at the dark - ness 'til

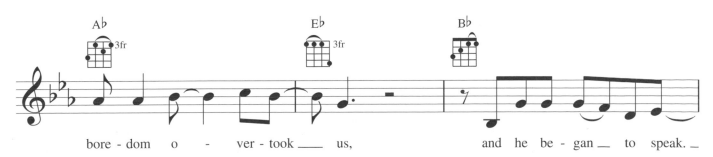

bore-dom o - ver-took __ us, and he be-gan __ to speak. __

know when to fold ____ 'em,   know when to walk _

____ a - way, _   and know when to run. ____ You nev - er

count your mon - ey   when you're sit - tin' at the ta -

- ble. There'll be time e - nough __ for count - in'

when the deal - in's done.

Verse

2. Ev - 'ry gam - bler knows _

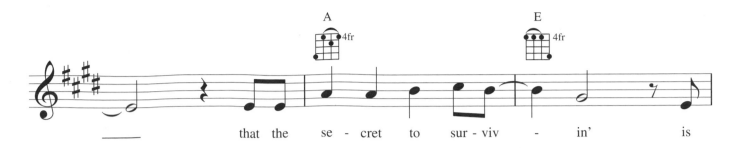

that the se - cret to sur - viv - in' is

know - in' what to throw a - way ___ and know - in' what to keep. ___

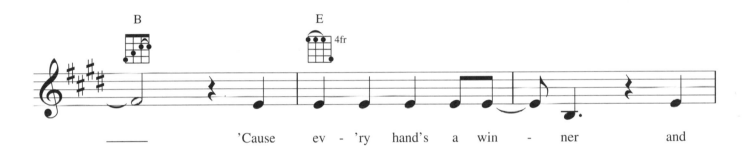

___ 'Cause ev - 'ry hand's a win - ner and

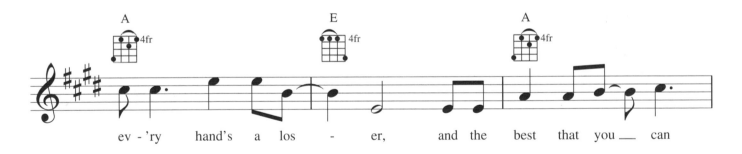

ev - 'ry hand's a los - er, and the best that you ___ can

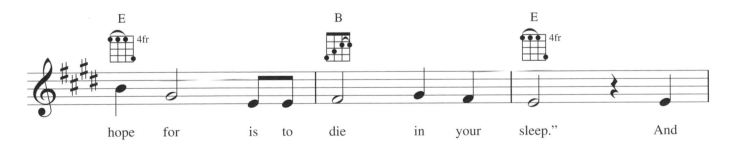

hope for is to die in your sleep." And

when he'd fin - ished speak - in', he turned back towards the win -

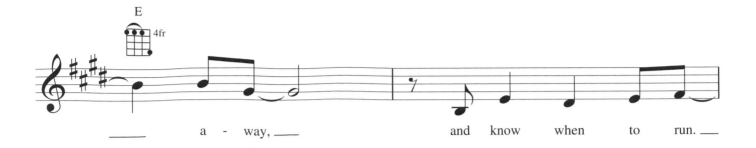

a - way, ___ and know when to run. __

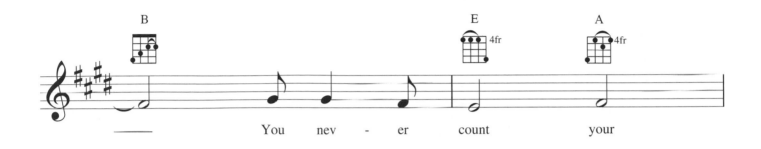

__ You nev - er count your

mon - ey when you're sit - tin' at the ta -

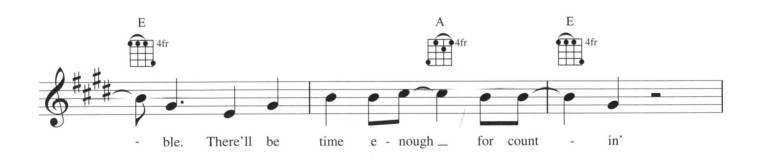

- ble. There'll be time e - nough __ for count - in'

when the deal - in's done. You got to done.

Green Green Grass of Home

Words and Music by Curly Putman

First note

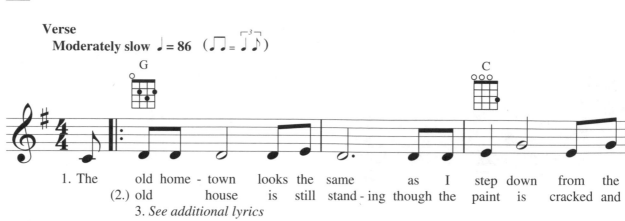

1. The old home - town looks the same as I step down from the
(2.) old house is still stand - ing though the paint is cracked and
3. *See additional lyrics*

train, and there to meet me was my ma - ma and
dry, and there's that old oak tree that I used to

pa - pa. Down the road I look and
play on. Down the lane I walk with

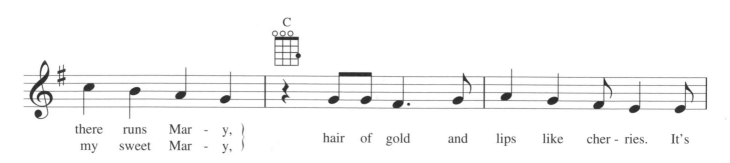

there runs Mar - y, } hair of gold and lips like cher - ries. It's
my sweet Mar - y, }

Additional Lyrics

3. *Spoken:* Then I awake, and look around me at the grey walls that surround me,
And I realize that I was only dreaming.
For there's a guard and there's a sad, old padre. Arm in arm we'll walk at daybreak.
Again I'll touch the green, green grass of home.

Heart and Soul

from the Paramount Short Subject A SONG IS BORN
Words by Frank Loesser
Music by Hoagy Carmichael

First note

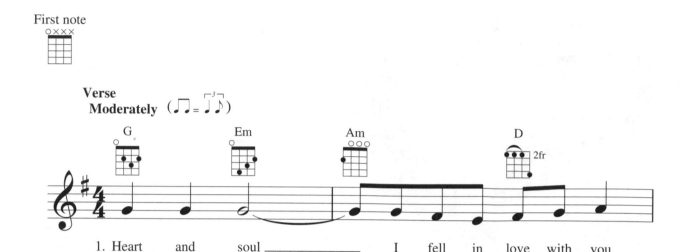

1. Heart and soul _____ I fell in love with you.
2. *See additional lyrics*

Heart and soul, _____ the way a fool would do.

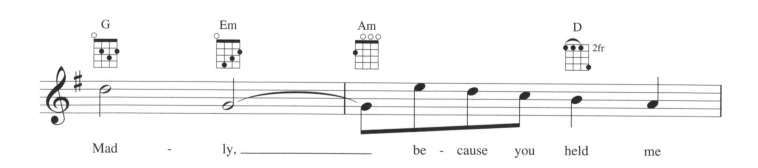

Mad - ly, _____ be - cause you held me

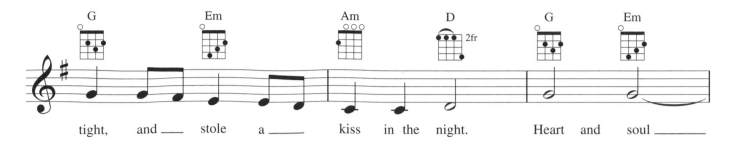

tight, and ___ stole a _____ kiss in the night. Heart and soul _____

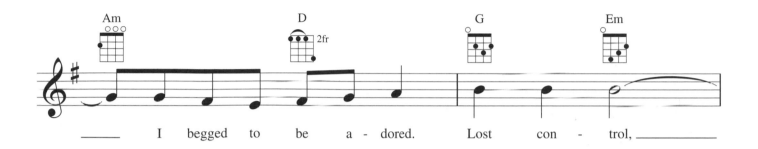

_____ I begged to be a - dored. Lost con - trol, _____

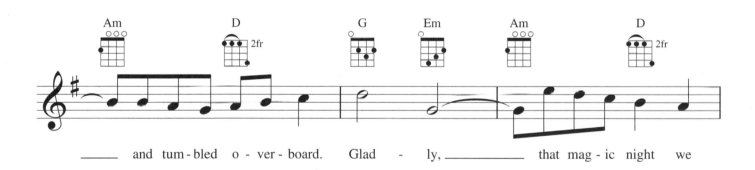

_____ and tum - bled o - ver - board. Glad - ly, _____ that mag - ic night we

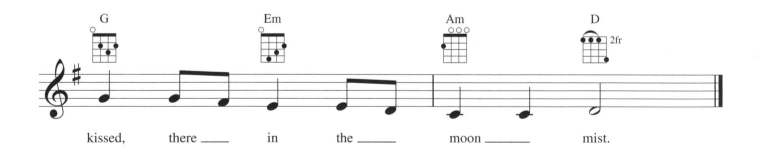

kissed, there ___ in the _____ moon _____ mist.

Additional Lyrics

2. But now I see,
   What one embrace can do.
   Look at me,
   It's got me loving you.
   Madly;
   That little kiss you stole,
   Held all my heart and soul.

Help Me Rhonda

Words and Music by Brian Wilson and Mike Love

First note

Verse
Medium Rock

1. Since she put me down I've been out do - in' in my head. ___
(2.) gon - na be my wife and I was gon - na be her man. ___

___ Come in late at night ___ and in the
___ But she let an - oth - er guy come be -

morn - in' I just lay in bed. ___ Well,
tween us and it shat - tered our plans. ___ Well,

Rhon - da, you look ___ so fine, _____ and I
Rhon - da, you caught ___ my eye, _____ and I'll

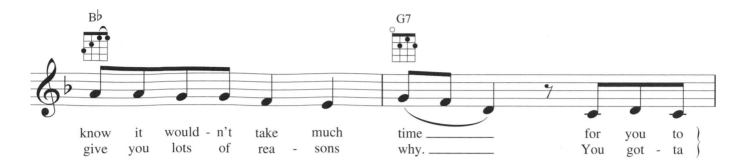

know it would-n't take much time _____ for you to
give you lots of rea - sons why. _____ You got - ta

help me, Rhon - da, help me get her out of my heart. ___

Chorus

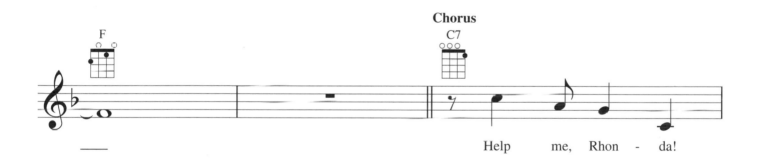

___ Help me, Rhon - da!

Help, help me, Rhon - da! Help me, Rhon - da! Help, help me, Rhon - da!

Help me, Rhon - da! Help, help me, Rhon - da! Help me, Rhon - da!

Help, help me, Rhon - da! Help me, Rhon - da! Help, help me, Rhon - da!

Help me, Rhon - da! Help, help me, Rhon - da! Help me, Rhon - da,

yeah, get her out of my heart. ____   2. She was

Help me, Rhon - da! Help, help me, Rhon - da!

Help me, Rhon - da! Help, help me, Rhon - da!

Hey, Soul Sister

Words and Music by Pat Monahan, Espen Lind and Amund Bjorkland

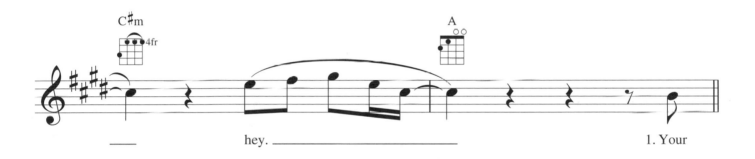

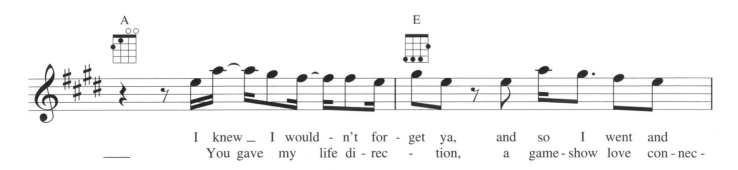

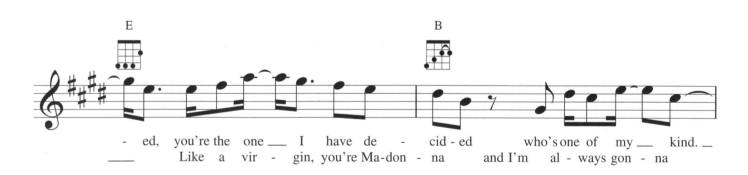

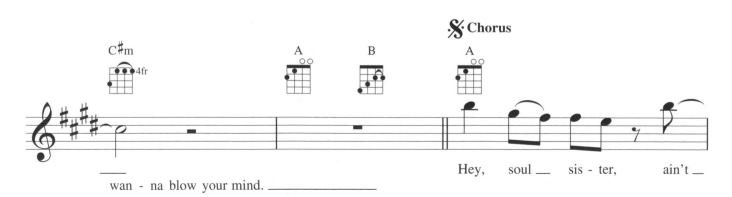

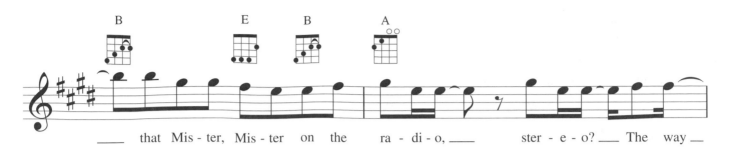

that Mis - ter, Mis - ter on the ra - di - o, ___ ster - e - o? ___ The way ___

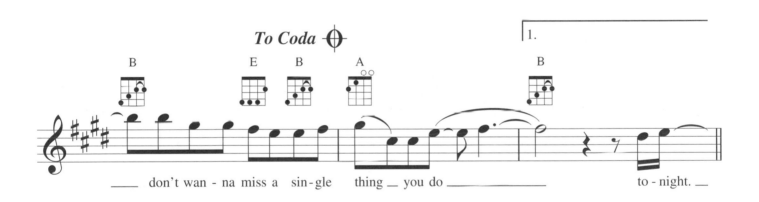

___ you move ___ ain't fair, you know. ___ Hey, ___ soul ___ sis - ter, I ___

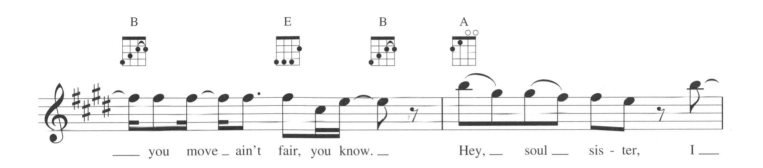

To Coda ⊕

1.

___ don't wan - na miss a sin - gle thing ___ you do ___ to - night. ___

Interlude

___ Hey, ___ hey, ___ hey. ___

2.

Verse

___ to - night. ___ 5. The way you can cut a rug, ___

watch - ing you's ___ the on - ly drug ___ I need. ___

___ Some gang - sta, I'm ___ so thug. ___ You're the

on - ly one ___ I'm dream - in' of. ___ You see,

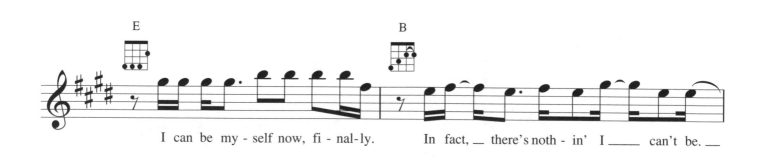

I can be my - self now, fi - nal - ly. In fact, ___ there's noth - in' I ___ can't be. ___

D.S. al Coda

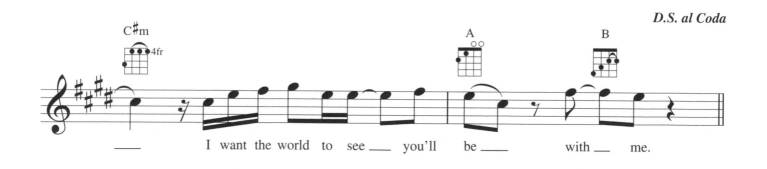

___ I want the world to see ___ you'll be ___ with ___ me.

Coda

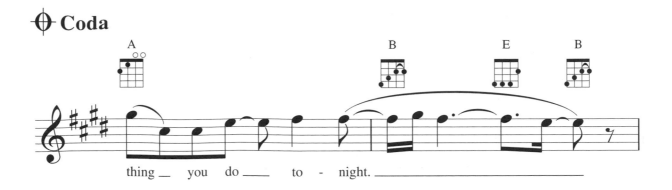

thing __ you do __ to - night. _____

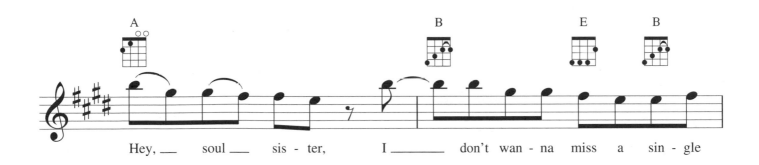

Hey, __ soul __ sis - ter, I _____ don't wan - na miss a sin - gle

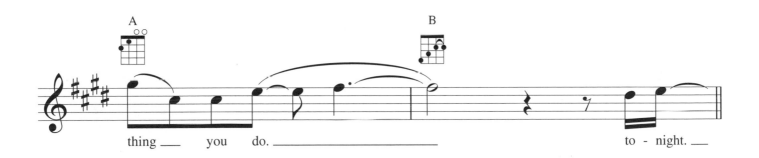

thing __ you do. _____ to - night. __

Outro

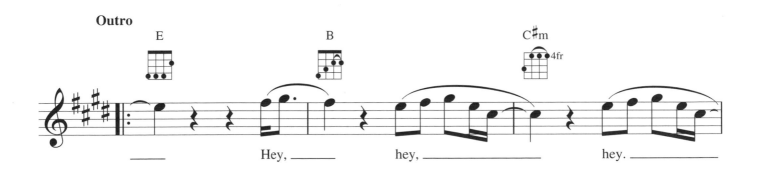

____ Hey, _____ hey, _____ hey. _____

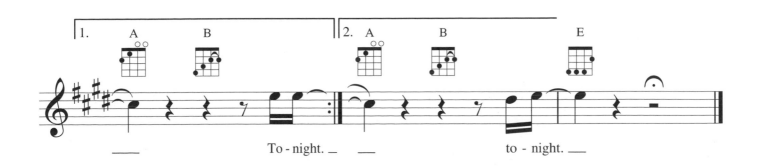

1. ____ To - night. __ __ 2. _____ to - night. __

Hey, Good Lookin'

Words and Music by Hank Williams

High Hopes

Words by Sammy Cahn
Music by James Van Heusen

Lover

from the Paramount Picture LOVE ME TONIGHT
Words by Lorenz Hart
Music by Richard Rodgers

The Hokey Pokey

Words and Music by Charles P. Macak, Tafft Baker and Larry LaPrise

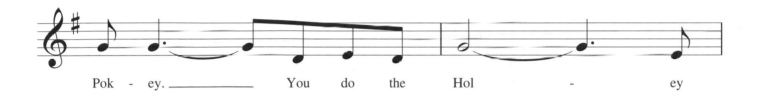

bout.   2. You put your   bout.   You do the Hok - ey

Pok - ey. _____ You do the Hol - ey

Pok - ey. _____ You do the Hok - ey

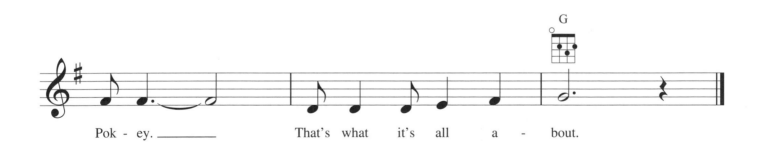

Pok - ey. _____   That's what it's all a - bout.

Additional Lyrics

2nd time: left foot	7th time: head
3rd time: right arm	8th time: right hip
4th time: left arm	9th time: left hip
5th time: right elbow	10th time: whole self
6th time: left elbow	

Performance Notes

All You Need Is Love (page 6)

On June 25, 1967, the first global television program, *Our World*, was broadcast via satellite to over 400 million viewers in 26 countries. The BBC commissioned the Beatles to write a song, which would serve as the United Kingdom's contribution. It needed to be simple, clear, and easily understood by everyone. Lennon rose to the task with "All You Need Is Love," which became one of the band's greatest peace anthems.

This song is in the key of G major and lays out very nicely on the uke. Notice that there are several alternative voicings for G during the first line. The only chord in the whole song that's not normally found in G major is the B7 chord in the chorus. You can hear how colorful it sounds when it's played, and John Lennon's melody makes the most of this with an ear-catching, chromatically ascending phrase at that point.

"All You Need Is Love" is unique for a pop song in that it contains mixed meters. No, this doesn't have anything to do with a pile of mixed up parking meters. A song's meter, or time signature, tells how many beats are in each measure. The most common time signature in pop music is 4/4, which means there are four quarter notes (beats) in each measure. You can count it "1–2–3–4, 1, 2, 3, 4." However, in "All You Need Is Love," measures of 3/4 are mixed in at the end of phrases. So you have to count the verses as "1–2–3–4, 1–2–3, 1–2–3–4, 1–2–3." On the chorus, the song returns to the more normal 4/4 meter. So be sure to keep your eye out for this bit of rhythmic trickery!

The song is also played with a *swing feel*. This is indicated by the ♪♪ = ♪♪ at the top of the music. This means that the eighth notes are not played evenly; the first is longer than the second. If you were to count each beat as "1–and–uh, 2–and–uh, 3–and–uh, 4–and–uh," with each syllable given equal duration, then the eighth notes in a swing feel would fall on the number and the "uh." It's easier to hear than it is to explain on paper, so be sure to listen to the original recording. By comparison, a song like "Just What I Needed" by The Cars is played with a normal (or straight) feel, where each eighth note is counted "1–and, 2–and, 3–and, 4–and."

Bali Ha'i (page 10)

Featured in the 1949 musical *South Pacific,* "Bali Ha'i" is a classic Rodgers and Hammerstein song with some very interesting harmony; Perry Como recorded it as a single. It tells the story of the mystical volcano island Bali Ha'i, which is near the main island on which the troops are stationed. The matriarch of the island, Bloody Mary, entices one of the officers with the mysterious song in hopes that he'll fall in love with her daughter.

Though the song is in the key of F major, there are almost as many non-diatonic chords as there are diatonic. *Diatonic* simply means in key, so *non-diatonic* means "not in the key." In Bali Ha'i, the non-diatonic chords are: E♭, A, G♭, F°7, E, D♭7, B♭+, and B♭m. Being out of key doesn't mean the chords sound bad — at least, not in the hands of such a skilled composer as Rodgers. But those chords are certainly more colorful and ear-catching than the diatonic ones like F, Gm7, C, and so on.

For the verse in the beginning, try strumming each chord once and then singing the lines in between. Alternatively, you could try *tremolo picking* each chord. This means you alternate down- and up-strokes as quickly as possible in an effort to create a steady bed of harmony over which to sing the phrases. Try to keep the wrist loose and lightly graze the strings. When the chorus arrives, you can continue with a more standard strumming pattern of one strum per beat.

If you want to tackle the melody on this song, you'll be playing many notes that don't fall within the F major scale. Notes that are . . . wait for it . . . non-diatonic. These non-diatonic notes are called *accidentals* and require a sharp, flat, or natural sign because they lie outside the key signature. In the case of this song, the key signature is F major, or one flat (B♭). So you'd normally play every B note as B♭. But notice right off the bat in the chorus, you have to play B♮. Keep an eye out for these and adjust the notes as necessary! Refer to the neck diagram at the end of the book when you need to.

(It's A) Beautiful Morning (page 12)

If you weren't aware of the fact that The Rascals enjoyed a huge hit with this song in 1968, you've no doubt heard it on T.V. commercials for Bounce fabric softener or the prescription drug Vioxx. This light, bouncy ode to optimism reached #3 on the Billboard charts and sold over a million copies for the group. The song sounds right at home on the uke and perfectly compliments the nature associated with the repertoire of the instrument.

"(It's A) Beautiful Morning" is in the key of F and contains almost all diatonic chords. However, there are a few interesting harmonies, such as C7sus4 and G7sus4, along with the sole non-diatonic chords, F+ and G7, that you'll need to watch out for.

This song is also played with a swing feel (see "All You Need Is Love"), so keep those eighth notes nice and bouncy. You want the feel of the strums to match the way the vocal melody sounds.

A nice strum pattern to use with this song is sometimes called the "boom chick-a." It alternates a quarter note with two eighth notes (swung, remember!). So you could count it as "1, 2–and, 3, 4–and," but saying "boom chick-a" is a little more fun!

In the bridge, you'll see the chord symbol "F+." This isn't an unfinished math problem. This stands for an F *augmented* chord. An augmented chord is a major chord with a raised 5th tone. F major is normally spelled F (1)–A(3)–C(5). But in F+, you raise the 5th tone, C, a half step to C♯. Notice that the chord shape in the grid is just like the F chord except that you're playing the third string (C) on the first fret instead, which makes it C♯.

Bibbidi-Bobbiddi-Boo (The Magic Song) *(page 18)*

Comprised of nonsense lyrics and a lilting beat, "Bibbidi-Bobbidi-Boo" was featured in Walt Disney's *Cinderella* in 1950, although a recording by Perry Como and the Fontane Sisters became the most popular version of the song. Want to know how to change a pumpkin into a carriage? Bibbidi-bobbidi-boo!

This song is played with a swing feel. This is very easy to hear with the abundance of triplets in the melody.

This song is in the key of F, and the chorus features only two chords: F and C7. These are the *tonic* and *dominant* and are built off the first and fifth degrees of the F major scale, respectively. The tonic and dominant are the most commonly used chords in music and help to clearly define the sound of a key. The dominant chord — C7 in this case — has a very strong pull back to the tonic, which is where it usually leads.

There are only five chords in this entire song, so it's a nice easy one to play on the uke. Have fun with it, keep it bouncy, and make sure you have room for the pumpkin chariot to appear in the room with you when you play it!

Blue Hawaii *(page 20)*

Though also made famous by Elvis Presley in the movie of the same name, "Blue Hawaii" originally appeared in the 1937 film *Waikiki Wedding*, which featured Bing Crosby. In it, pineapple company publicist Tony Marvin (Crosby) sets out to generate interest by sponsoring a "Miss Pineapple Princess" pageant, with the winner receiving an all-expense paid trip to the aloha state. Some mayhem ensues, but in the end, Marvin gets the girl, and all is well.

"Blue Hawaii" is a slow, graceful ballad played with a swing feel in the key of G major. A strum pattern of straight quarter notes or straight eighth notes will work nicely. Just remember to slightly accent (strum louder) the downbeats if you strum eighth notes.

The harmony in this song contains many common elements found in standards and pop songs. One such device is the *secondary dominant*. This is a non-diatonic chord that temporarily leads to another chord, which is usually (but not always) diatonic. In the key of G, the vi chord is normally Em. But in measure 4, we see the secondary dominant E7, which temporarily acts as the V chord to the following A chord. This is a bit of double trouble as well, because, although Am normally appears in the key of G, it's made A7 here — another secondary dominant that temporarily leads to the true dominant (V chord) of the key, D7.

When chords cycle like this — when the roots move down by a 5th (E down to A down to D down to G) — it's called a cycle of 5ths. Alternatively, you may see this called a cycle of 4ths, because the roots could also be seen as moving up a 4th.

You'll get lots of practice with seventh chords in this song, and watch out especially for the D7#5 at the end of the bridge! Don't worry, though; it's easier to play than it sounds.

Brown Eyed Girl *(page 15)*

One of the most popular rock 'n' roll songs of the 20th century and still heard daily via radio, DJ, or wedding band, "Brown Eyed Girl" was responsible for launching the solo career of Van Morrison. He wrote and recorded the song in 1967 for his debut album *Blowin' Your Mind*, immediately following the breakup of the Belfast group Them, and the single quickly rose to #10 on the Billboard charts. But for all its enduring success, it's also a cautionary tale. Due to hastily signing a solo recording contract without reading it or seeking legal advice, Van Morrison has stated that he's never received one red cent in royalties for penning or recording this classic. The moral of the story: Use those brown eyes to read everything before you sign on the dotted line!

This fun-loving gem is in the key of G major and is mostly comprised of three chords: G, C, and D — the backbone of hundreds if not thousands of hits throughout the years. These chords are the I, IV, and V chords in the key of G. The only other chord in the song is the vi chord, Em, which appears once in the chorus.

To propel this song properly, try strumming in eighth notes while accenting the *backbeat*; that's beats 2 and 4. So you could try counting it "1–and **2**–and 3–and **4**–and" to get used to the idea. This will simulate the backbeat of the snare drum and help get people's feet tapping.

Though it's not notated here, the signature intro dyad (that's instrument jargon for two notes played simultaneously) lick can easily be adapted to the uke and is not terribly difficult to figure out. Once you learn it for the G chord, simply slide it up five frets for the C chord. For instance, the first dyad, G/B, is simply the notes on strings 1 and 2 of your G chord.

Bye Bye Blackbird *(page 22)*

An enduring standard originally recorded by Gene Austin in 1926, it's often speculated that "Bye Bye Blackbird" tells the tale of a prostitute that's leaving the business and returning to her home. Countless versions of the song have been recorded throughout the years, including John Coltrane's version in 1981, for which he won a GRAMMY® award for Best Jazz Instrumental Performance. Other notable versions include those by Julie London, Miles Davis, Joe Cocker, and Peggy Lee. The song has been featured numerous films as well, including *Sleepless in Seattle, Public Enemies,* and *A River Runs Through It,* among others.

Like many jazz standards, "Bye Bye Blackbird" is composed in a 32-bar form. Though the most common arrangement of material in this form is AABA — two statements of a similar theme, one statement of contrasting material, and another statement similar to the first two, all eight measures in length — there are many variations on this, as is evidenced in this song, which is arranged in one 16-bar phrase, one 8-bar phrase, and another 8-bar phrase.

Though the melody here is notated in predominantly quarter notes, half notes, and whole notes, you'll rarely hear someone sing (or play) it exactly like this. In fact, if you were to program the notes into a computer and have them play exactly what's written here, it would sound pretty square. So, if you plan to croon (or just play the melody on the uke) feel free to take some liberty with where you start and end the phrases after you become comfortable with what's written. Listen to a few different versions of this song to hear what I mean.

Jazz makes abundant use of sophisticated harmonies, such as seventh chords, ninth chords, or sixth chords. You may not be familiar with all of the voicings here, so take a minute to scan through them first. Though you could get by without playing all the specific variations (7ths, 6ths, and so on), all those details give this music its charm and character.

Can't Help Falling in Love (page 24)

"Can't Help Falling in Love" is one of the most famous and widely covered Elvis ballads of all. Originally featured in the 1961 film *Blue Hawaii* (starring Elvis), the King began to close out his performances with it beginning in the late 1960s. The British reggae troop UB40 also enjoyed a #1 Billboard hit with it in 1993, and it's been covered by artists as diverse as U2, Perry Como, Harry Connick, Jr., Rick Astley, Richard Marx, and dozens more throughout the years. You can hear a version from the A-Teens featured prominently in Disney's animated film *Lilo and Stitch*.

"Can't Help Falling in Love" is written with a 12/8 time signature. This means that there are 12 beats in a measure, and an eighth note is counted as the beat. The first, fourth, seventh, and tenth eighth notes are usually accented, so you could count it like this: "1–2–3, 4–5–6, 7–8–9, 10–11–12." Some like to count it simply with four beats using a triplet undercurrent, such as this: "1–and–uh, 2–and–uh, 3–and–uh, 4–and–uh." Regardless, just remember that it basically involves four beats or pulses per measure that are divided into three equal parts.

In 12/8 ballads such as this one, a very common accompaniment involves arpeggiating the chord. An *arpeggio* is simply the notes of a chord played in succession rather than all at once. So you might try playing through the strings in a pattern of "4–3–2, 1–2–3, 4–3–2, 1–2–3" for each chord. Or you could use other arpeggio patterns as well. This one happens to work nicely in 12/8 because it lines up with each triplet beat.

The brackets toward the end with the "1." And "2." beneath them are *first* and *second endings*. When you see these symbols, play through the "1." bracket until you reach the end repeat sign. Then go back to the opening repeat sign and start again. This time, when you reach the "1." bracket, skip over it to the "2." bracket and continue on from there.

Coconut (page 26)

"Coconut" is a song written and recorded by Harry Nilsson and first featured on his 1971 album *Nilsson Schmilsson*. Younger audiences are no doubt more familiar with the slightly modified version of the song appearing in a commercial for Coca Cola, in which the lyrics are modified to "You put the lime in the Coke you nut," or the song's appearance in several television shows, including *House* and *Bones*. Though he never reached the mass level of superstardom enjoyed by his friends, colleagues, and admirers The Beatles, Nilsson was a seminal music figure in the 1960s and 1970s, a talented singer and songwriter, and a winner of two GRAMMY awards.

"Coconut" is literally a one-chord song; it consists of nothing but C7 throughout its entirety. Therefore, in order to keep things interesting, it helps to really get into the goofy character of the lyrics. Have fun with it and don't take yourself too seriously! Nilsson injected many of his songs with a healthy sense of humor, and this song is a prime example.

If you'd like to try your hand (nice pun, huh?) at playing this melody on the uke, you'll be encountering many blue notes. These are non-diatonic notes that generally lend a bluesy sound to music. "Coconut" is in the key of C, but you'll see a few notes appear frequently that don't normally occur within the C major scale. In the verse, these are the notes D♯ (which is also represented *enharmonically* as E♭) and F♯. Notice that the F♯ is always used as a passing tone between F and G. The chorus also makes prominent use of the note B♭, which is found in a C7 chord but not in the C major scale.

'Deed I Do (page 33)

"'Deed I Do" is a swingin' jazz standard composed by Fred Rose (music) and Walter Hirsch (lyrics) originally recorded in 1926 by S.L. Stambaugh and Ben Bernie, although Ruth Etting had a top ten hit with the song in 1927. Clarinetist Benny Goodman also covered the song as his debut recording. It's a light, fun song with a simple message: "Do I love you? 'Deed I do!"

"'Deed I Do" sounds in the key of C and is a typical 32-bar song in the standard AABA format. After two statements of the 8-bar A section with slightly different lyrics, the bridge (B section, or middle eight) begins on the IV chord — a very common harmonic maneuver. The A section is then reprised once again for the final eight measures of the form. When performing songs such as this, jazz musicians will often take solos over the entire form after the melody has been stated and then return to the melody once more to close out the song.

Also notice the abundance of the Dm7–G7–C progression in this song. This is a ii–V–I progression, which is perhaps the most prevalent chord progression in all of jazz. It's often heard at the end of a section to solidify the key before another statement of the same theme. This is exactly what it's doing during the first ending in measures 7–8. Notice, however, that the second ending doesn't contain this progression, because it wouldn't properly lead to the F chord that starts the bridge.

This song is played with a swing feel. See "All You Need Is Love" if you need a refresher on what this means. There have been uptempo versions of this song as well as moderate versions, so listen to several different ones to see which feels best to you.

Try strumming quarter notes with the second and fourth slightly more staccato than the first and third. *Staccato* is music jargon for short, crisp, or abbreviated. The faster the tempo, the more staccato these will be. With practice, you can really make something swing this way.

Dream a Little Dream of Me (page 34)

Another standard from the 1930s, "Dream a Little Dream of Me" was first recorded by Ozzie Nelson and His Orchestra in 1931. Since then, it's been done by just about everyone, including Ella Fitzgerald, Louis Jordan, Dinah Shore, Bing Crosy and Georgia Gibbs (duet), Dean Martin, Nat King Cole, Doris Day, and more. "Mama" Cass Elliot also enjoyed a #12 hit with the song in 1968. Although it was released as a solo effort (much to bandmate's John Phillips' dismay), the record actually featured all members of the Mamas & the Papas.

"Dream a Little Dream of Me" is shown here in the key of G major and features many different chords. The ii–V–I progression (see "'Deed I Do") is seen here in numerous keys, briefly *tonicizing* other keys, as it often the case in jazz. Although you're in the key of G, you see ii–V progressions also in the keys of Am (Bm7♭5–E7–Am, measures 4–5) and E♭ (measures 10–11, Fm7–B♭7–E♭). Notice that, though the tonicization of Am is extremely brief (only one measure), the tonicization of E♭ lasts throughout the entire bridge, clearly classifying as a key change to E♭ major. The Am7–D7 at the end of the bridge leads you back to the key of G for the final 8-bar statement in the form.

This song is played with a swing feel (see "All You Need Is Love"). It's usually performed at slow to moderate tempo, though feel free to experiment in this regard.

Be sure to scan through the chords for ones with which you're not familiar before you start through the song. There are a lot of chromatic notes in the melody as well, so you may want to play through it on the uke or maybe a piano if you plan to sing it. Listening to other versions is another option, but keep in mind that each performer often takes a liberty with the melody.

Easter Parade (page 36)

"Easter Parade" is an Irvin Berlin composition first introduced in 1933 for a Broadway musical called *As Thousands Cheer*. Subsequent versions include one by Bing Crosby for the film *Holiday Inn* (1942) and Judy Garland for the film *Easter Parade* (1948). Interestingly, Irving Berlin actually wrote the melody for the song in 1917 with different lyrics, but after the song ("Smile and Show Me Your Dimple") went unsuccessful, he recast it for "Easter Parade." A joyful tune that talks of bonnets, clovers, and sonnets on Fifth Avenue, it's quite enjoyable to play on the uke.

"Easter Parade" follows the 32-bar form AABA structure (see "'Deed I Do") in the key of C. Instead of beginning the bridge (B section) on the IV chord though, as is quite often the case, it begins with a dominant I chord (C7), which is also another common device. This acts as a secondary dominant (see "Blue Hawaii") that leads to the IV chord. It's also common to begin with a minor v chord (Gm in this case) followed by a dominant I chord. This is essentially creating a temporary ii–V progression of the IV chord (F).

In measure 21, you'll see a natural sign on the D note in the melody. But the key signature for this song is C major (no sharps or flats) — so why do you need the natural on the D? This is what's known as a courtesy accidental, and it's there to remind you that D should in fact be natural after playing a D♯ in the previous measure. It's just a little "common courtesy."

This song is meant to describe all the grandeur of a New York parade. Therefore, it's usually lavishly orchestrated with lots of instrumental flourishes and ear candy. To recreate some of that energy, try mixing up your strum patterns by maybe throwing a few sixteenth-note strums in between the vocal phrases. Or you could try interjecting a few abrupt rests for a beat here and there. Anything that provides a jolt of interest will be a welcome addition to this song.

Edelweiss (page 38)

Originally written for the 1959 Broadway musical *The Sound of Music,* and later appearing in the 1965 film of the same name starring Julie Andrews and Christopher Plummer, "Edelweiss" is actually the last song ever composed by the lauded team of Rodgers and Hammerstein. (Oscar Hammerstein succumbed to stomach cancer nine months after the stage musical opened.) Named after a striking white flower that grows high in the Alps, the song is an ode to Austria during the time of the oppressive Nazi regime. It's a flowing waltz in the key of C that effortlessly conjures images of beautiful, rolling mountains.

Like all waltzes, "Edelweiss" is written with a 3/4 time signature. This means each measure contains three beats, and the quarter note is counted as the beat. The first beat of each measure is accented, so the count sounds like "1–2–3, 1–2–3."

"Edelweiss" follows the standard 32-bar AABA form (see "'Deed I Do") and contains almost all diatonic chords in the key of C. In this arrangement (though others may differ), the only two non-diatonic chords (see "Bali Ha'i") are Gm6 and Fm, both found in the final restatement of the A section the last eight measures of the song).

The tempo indication here says "Slowly, With Expression." The composer or arranger doesn't just put that information up there for fun. Keep these indications in mind when performing the song if you want to convey the intended spirit of the song. Picture snow-capped mountaintops, and throw in a mountain goat if you'd like (optional).

On other instruments, such as guitar and piano, waltz accompaniment often involves a pattern of bass note–chord–chord, bass note–chord–chord, and so on. On the uke, this can work too, but you have to remember that string 4 isn't the lowest pitched string. So if you want to try that pattern, try playing a pattern of string 3–full chord–full chord, and so on. Alternately, you can just strum quarter notes, accenting the first beat by strumming a bit harder. Whichever you choose, strive for a flowing sound in your strums.

Eleanor Rigby (page 40)

A standout track on the pivotal *Revolver* album, "Eleanor Rigby" is a McCartney song that features a double string quartet as the only accompaniment, similar to "Yesterday." Though McCartney can remember other specific inspirations for the names "Eleanor" and "Rigby," it's interesting to note that a gravestone with the name "Eleanor Rigby" was discovered in a graveyard within earshot of where McCartney and Lennon first met. Since then, McCartney has supposed that his attraction to the name could have been a product of his subconscious memory of that grave. A tale of loneliness and despair, its haunting melody and brilliant string arrangement by producer Sir George Martin have made it an enduring fan favorite.

"Eleanor Rigby" is in the key of E minor and is comprised primarily of two chords: C and Em — the ♭VI and i chords, respectively. Though you could perform an acceptable version of the song using only those two chords, the song sounds much more sophisticated when the other harmonic details are included. These additional chords are found in the chorus and include Em7, Em6, and Cmaj7. Notice that the progression of Em7–Em6–Cmaj7 produces one chromatically descending line on string 3 while all other notes of the chords remain the same.

The text "D.C. al Coda" appearing at the end of the second ending is short for "Da Capo al Coda." "Da Capo" is Italian for "from the head," and "al Coda" is Italian for "to the coda." This is a routing direction that saves composers and copyists from having to rewrite music. This was much more important during the days before a simple mouse click can copy and paste a novel for us. But they're still used today to save ink and paper. This direction is telling you to return to the "head" of the song — the top or beginning — and play through until you reach the "To Coda" indication. This can be seen just before the first ending bracket. At that point, you jump directly to the Coda for the final Em chord.

A strum pattern of straight quarter notes works surprisingly well for the verses of this song on the uke. Feel free to try eighth note strumming in the chorus to mix it up.

Five Foot Two, Eyes of Blue (Has Anybody Seen My Girl?) (page 42)

"Five Foot Two, Eyes of Blue (Has Anybody Seen My Girl?)" is a 1920s song originally recorded by The California Ramblers in 1925 for their self-titled album. It's also appeared under the name "Has Anybody Seen My Gal?" and other variations as well. Cover versions throughout the years include those by Shane Fenton and the Fentones, Mitch Miller, and Milla Jovovich. It's a fun, simple song with silly lyrics — great to whip out when people are ready to cut loose and have some fun.

This song is written in cut time, which is indicated by the ¢ symbol. This is reserved for songs with a fast tempo that are counted at half the speed. This is why the tempo indication given says that a half note = 100, as opposed to the more common quarter note. (The term "in 2," which appears after "Moderately," is another way of saying cut time.) All this basically just means that when you tap your foot to the music and count the beats, you count two half-note beats for every measure as opposed to four, super fast quarter note beats.

Notice also the abundance of secondary dominant chords here (see "Blue Hawaii"). The song's in the key of C, but it also includes E7, A7, and D7, all of which are secondary dominants. In the bridge, you see a very common cycle of 5ths progression (see "Blue Hawaii") that begins on the III chord, E7, and continues cycling up a 5th, A7–D7–G7, until you arrive back at the tonic C for the last verse.

In the D.C. al Coda routing direction (see "Eleanor Rigby" for more on Coda roadmaps), notice that it says "take repeat." This type of information is included if you pass through a repeated section of music while on your way to the "To Coda" indication. In this case, you do, and so this is telling us to:

✔ Go back to the top (Capo), play through the first ending

✔ Go back to the top again, skip the first ending and play from the second ending

✔ Once you reach the "To Coda" indication, skip to the coda

Feel a little bossed around?

The Fool on the Hill (page 44)

"The Fool on the Hill" was a McCartney contribution from the *Magical Mystery Tour* album of 1967. In Paul's words, the song was written about Maharishi Mahesh Yogi and the ridicule that he often endured because of his giggling nature. It was one of John Lennon's favorite of Paul's songs, and he cited it as proof that Paul could write a "complete" song in a 1980 *Playboy* interview. The band shot a promotional video for the song near Nice, France at the end of October, 1967. Oh, the hardships of being a successful musician!

"Fool on the Hill" is a bit unusual for a pop song in that its tonic chord is a sixth chord. A sixth chord is a major triad with an added 6th tone. In this case, you have a D6 chord, which is spelled D (1)–F♯ (3)–A (5)–B (6). It's a more sophisticated sound than a major triad, but it's not quite as jazzy as a major seventh chord. But that's not the only bit of harmonic interest in the song.

For the chorus of the song, the key changes to D minor. This is what's known as the *parallel minor* of D major. This casts a darker tone to the music that's immediately apparent and quite striking. A parallel minor shares the same tonic as its parallel major, but the rest of the notes in the scale are different.

A D major scale is spelled D–E–F♯–G–A–B–C♯, but the parallel D minor is spelled D–E–F–G–A–B♭–C. A *relative minor*, which is more common, shares the same notes as its relative major, but the tonic is different. The relative minor of D major is B minor, which is spelled B–C♯–D–E–F♯–G–A. If you notice, those are the same notes as found in D major; only B is treated as the tonic.

In the original piano accompaniment for this song, Paul plays a quarter-note accompaniment pattern. Strumming the same way sounds great on the uke.

The Gambler *(page 47)*

Kenny Rogers scored a huge hit with this title track from his 1978 album *The Gambler* and won a GRAMMY for best male country vocal performance in the process. Written by Don Schlitz, the song tells the story of a dispirited Rogers receiving advice from a mysterious gambler on a train "bound for nowhere." For a swig of Rogers' whisky, the gambler agrees to give him the secret of his success in "making a life out of readin' people's faces." Caution is advised though; don't try your hand in Vegas after listening to the lyrics of this song, because it's not exactly a goldmine of instruction. Let's just say I hope Kenny wasn't all that thirsty anymore!

"The Gambler" is written in cut time (see "Five Foot Two, Eyes of Blue"), which means you count the song in two beats for every measure.

The song is presented here in its original key of E♭ major. This is a "I, IV, V" song containing the chords E♭, A♭, and B♭. On the ukulele, this means that you'll be playing barre chords exclusively. Luckily, barring isn't too difficult on the uke, and it shouldn't take too much time to get it down if you're not familiar with it. Notice that, for both the E♭ and A♭ chords, your first finger will be barring the third fret. You'll only need to move from this position for the B♭ chord.

On the original recording, the accompaniment is primarily provided by a guitar played in finger picking fashion. This would sound nice on the uke played the same way. Try placing your thumb on string 4 and your index and ring fingers on strings 2 and 1, respectively. Then play steady eighth notes in a pattern of string 4–string 2–string 3–string 1, with your thumb alternating to handle both string 4 and string 3. Or you could try *rolling string patterns*, such as 4–3–2–1 or 4–1–2–3, both of which would involve bringing your ring finger into play on string 1 and moving your index and middle over one string.

Green Green Grass of Home *(page 54)*

"Green Green Grass of Home" was first made popular in 1965 by Porter Wagoner; Bobby Bare also had a hit with the song that same year. Subsequent versions include those by Charlie Pride, Johnny Cash, Hank Snow, Joan Baez, Merle Haggard, Elvis Presley, Kenny Rogers, and Gram Parsons. Initially, the song seems to tell the story of a man returning home for the first time since leaving as a child, greeted by his parents, his beloved, and friends. It's a joyful homecoming filled with pleasant childhood memories restored and hope for a bright future. However, it's soon revealed that this was all a dream, and the narrator is actually on death row and scheduled to be executed that morning. Talk about a cold shot of reality!

"Green Green Grass of Home" is played at a moderate tempo with a swing feel. This one should bounce along gracefully, but not too slowly.

Try strumming this song with a "boom chick-a" pattern. See "(It's A) Beautiful Morning" for more on this pattern.

This is another three-chord song in the key of G major that uses only the I, IV, and V chords. In this case, that means G (I), C (IV), and D7 (V). It's simple, but it's all that's necessary for this song!

Heart and Soul (*page 56*)

If you can't play the piano, there are two songs that you'll likely still be able to peck out. One is "Chopsticks," and the other is "Heart and Soul." The latter is often taught as a duet, with one plunking out the chords and the other stringing together the melody — often with one finger! The song was originally performed by Larry Clinton & His Orchestra featuring Bea Wain in 1938. Since then, it's been covered dozens of times by artists as diverse as Floyd Cramer, Ella Fitzgerald, Crystal Gale, Dean Martin, Mel Tormé, and many more. Of course, the song was also featured in the movie *Big*, in which actors Tom Hanks and Robert Loggia performed an instrumental version by stepping on a giant piano keyboard. For their encore performance, they followed the song with what else? "Chopsticks"!

 Although the song is often learned with a I–vi–IV–V chord progression, which has come to be known as the 1950s progression because of its prevalence in so many doo-wop hits of the day, the original version made use of a I–vi–ii–V progression — much more common in the jazz world. In the key of G, this translates to G–Em–Am–D, though most jazzers will often dress it up with seventh chords or other extended harmonies.

In case you lived under a rock and don't have the sound of this chord progression drilled into your head, "Heart and Soul" is played with a swing feel and should bounce with childlike enthusiasm.

 Try playing this song by strumming continuous eighth notes (remember to make them swing!). For extra credit, try accenting the backbeat, or beats 2 and 4 (see "Brown Eyed Girl"), to really make the song come to life.

Help Me Rhonda (*page 58*)

"Help Me Rhonda," originally appearing on their 1965 album *Today!*, was one of several #1 hits for the Beach Boys — the first being "I Get Around." The most popular version of the song, however, is a re-recorded single version that was released a month after the album. Written by Brian Wilson and Mike Love, the song tells the story of a man pleading with Rhonda to help him cure his recently broken heart. For avid Beach Boys fans, it's interesting to note that an incident occurred during the recording of this song involving an altercation between Brian Wilson and father Murray Wilson. The entire event, lasting nearly ten minutes, was recorded on tape and can be heard at various online sources.

"Help Me Rhonda" is a medium rock 'n' roll song played with a swing feel, so be sure to let the eighth notes sound nice and bouncy.

 This song is in the key of F and consists mostly of the I (F) and V (C7) chords. However, several other diatonic chords come into play, such as iv (Dm), IV (B♭), and ii (Gm7). There's also a G7 chord that occurs near the end of the verse. Because this is a non-diatonic chord, it's classified as a secondary dominant chord (see "Blue Hawaii"). However, this chord doesn't resolve up a 5th (to C) as expected; it actually leads to the I chord (F). Therefore, it's further classified as a nonfunctional (or non-resolving) secondary dominant.

Try strumming eighth notes (remember to swing!) with an accent on beats 2 and 4, or the backbeat. You want this song to roll along briskly but not race away.

Hey, Good Lookin' *(page 66)*

This classic old-style country tune was written and recorded by Hank Williams in 1951, resulting in a #1 hit for ol' Hank. Fifty years later, in 2001, it was inducted into the GRAMMY Hall of Fame. Since then, there have been more cover versions than you can shake a stick at, including those by The Mavericks, Jimmy Buffet (featuring Clint Black, George Strait, Alan Jackson, Toby Keith, and Kenny Chesney), Johnny Cash, and Linda Ronstadt. It's a simple, fun song that pretty much sums up Western civilization as we know it: A guy trying to get a girl.

"Hey Good Lookin'" is notated in cut time (see "Five Foot Two, Eyes of Blue"), so you don't need to stomp your foot on every beat (unless you just want to). Count the song as "1, 2, 1, 2," and so on.

This tune is in the key of C and consists mostly of three chords: C, D7, and G7. Notice that the D7 is a secondary dominant (see "Blue Hawaii"), as Dm would normally be diatonic to the key of C. In the bridge, move to the IV chord (F), which is an extremely common maneuver for the middle eight.

"Hey Good Lookin'" follows the standard 32-bar AABA form that so many songs from the 1950s and earlier do.

The "boom chick-a" strum pattern will work perfectly for this song (see "(It's a) Beautiful Morning"), and remember to swing those eighth notes. It should be noted that this song, though usually performed at a fairly brisk tempo, works quite nicely at moderate tempos as well. Regardless of which tempo you decide on, the chords change slowly enough, making your frethand job fairly easy on this one.

Hey, Soul Sister *(page 61)*

For fans of Train's earlier rootsy rock, a pop ditty like "Hey, Soul Sister" came as a bit of a surprise. After all, the main accompaniment takes place on . . . ahem . . . a ukulele! You can't argue with the band's decision to venture down the more pop side of things, though, when you look at the numbers generated by this song. By far their most successful single, it hit #3 on the Billboard charts and has sold over 5 million digital copies in the U.S. alone. It's the eighth most downloaded song in history and was the top-selling song on iTunes in 2010. An ode to love at first sight, the song quotes several nods to 1980s culture, including Mister Mister, Madonna's "Like a Virgin," and the "radio stereo" (I guess iPod just didn't sing as well).

The backbone of this song is built upon a I–V–vi–IV progression in the key of E, which translates to E–B–C#m–A. If the I–iv–IV–V progression can be called the 1950s progression, then the I–V–vi–IV could be called the from-1980s-on progression. It's been the backbone for countless hits, including Journey's "Don't Stop Believing," U2's "With or Without You," Jason Mraz's "I'm Yours," Richard Marx's "Right Here Waiting," Maroon 5's "She Will Be Loved," and on an on.

Remember that "Hey, Soul Sister" is played with a swing feel. But wait, you say! That swing symbol looks different. Your eyes don't deceive you! This is played with *swung sixteenth* notes in stead of swung eighth notes. It's kind of like you're playing a swung eighth note groove twice as fast. Listen to the track if that sounds confusing. After all, the song is played on the uke!

Regarding the strum pattern, do I really have to say it again? Check out the song! If you're really that stubborn, here's the strum pattern: 8th-16th-16th, 16th-16th-16th-16th. That's the two-beat pattern that pretty much runs through the length of the song.

High Hopes (page 68)

"High Hopes" was first performed by Frank Sinatra in 1959 for the film *A Hole in the Head*. It was nominated for a Grammy and won an Oscar for Best Original Song at the Academy Awards. A whimsical song that gives examples in the animal kingdom of unimaginable feats for those feeling down in the dumps, the song was also featured on Sinatra's 1961 album *All the Way*, where he performed with a children's choir. You may also recognize Doris Day's rendition of the song from the 1998 animated film *Antz*. The song has also been adopted by New York Phillies fans and is sung after every win at their home stadium.

"High Hopes" is in the key of C and makes generous use of the I–vi–ii–V progression (C–Am–Dm–G7 in this case), but it also features another chord commonly heard in jazzier songs: the diminished seventh chord. Notice in the verse how the first chord, C, is connected to the third chord, Dm, by a C#°7 chord. This creates a chromatically ascending movement of C–C#–D. In this case, the C#°7 chord is actually acting as a substitute for A7, which would be a secondary dominant. In fact, A7 and C#°7 share 3 out of their four notes: C#, E, and G.

The song does feature a strong secondary dominant in the chorus in the form of D7, which resolves as expected to the true V chord of the key, G7.

Play this song with a bouncy swing feel. The tempo isn't too fast, but it should be spirited.

Check out the original recordings of this song to get an idea how to strum. There are several spots where the music stops dynamically, and it really does add some excitement.

The Hokey Pokey (page 74)

Heard in skating rinks, kids parties, and dances around the world, the famous "Hokey Pokey" was originally popularized in the U.S. during the 1950s with a recording by the Ram Trio. There is some debate as to who was responsible for creating the dance that accompanies the song, but it has become fairly standardized in the U.S. at this point. In short, people stand in a circle and put in, take out, and shake about various body parts. And that's what it's all about.

There are exactly two chords in this song: I and V. In the key of G, this means G and D7. One interesting thing to note is the use of a blues note (see "Coconut") in the melody over the V chord. It's notated here as an E#, which is enharmonic for the more commonly used F♮. E# is used is to avoid having so many accidentals in the same measure.

"The Hokey Pokey" is played with a swing feel and is notated in cut time. You'll be tapping your foot to what would be the alternating bass line (played by a bass, tuba, or other novelty instrument) on a fully orchestrated version of the song.

There is actually a chorus to this song, with which some might not be familiar, as it's not always performed. Be sure to give it a look through if it looks new to you.

Lover *(page 71)*

"Lover" is a composition by Richard Rodgers (music) and Lorenz Hart (lyrics). It was originally featured in the 1932 movie *Love Me Tonight,* starring Maurice Chevalier and Jeanette MacDonald. The film also contained several other Rodgers and Hart classics, including "Love Me Tonight," "Isn't It Romantic," and "Mimi." Interestingly, the song "Lover" is not set to a romantic scene at all, but a comic one in which Jeanette MacDonald attempts to tame a wild horse. Les Paul also released an instrumental guitar version of the song in 1948 for Capital Records.

The melody of "Lover" is highly chromatic in the verse, slowly and steadily descending from the tonic C to G with half-step neighbor notes throughout. This is accompanied by a series of ii–V progressions (see "'Deed I Do") that never resolve to their respective I chord: F#m–B7 (ii–V of E), Fm–Bb7 (ii–V of Eb), Em–A7 (ii–V of D), and Ebm–Ab7 (ii–V of Db). This gives way finally to the true ii–V of the key, Dm–G7, which does resolve to the tonic C chord. This stringing of ii–V progressions is a common practice in jazz and standards of this era.

The bridge modulates to E major with a repeating E–F#–B7 (I–ii–V in E) progression and then transposes much of the same material up to G for the second half with a G–Am–D7 progression, though the phrase changes course midway through the tonicization of G to lead back to C with a Dm–G7 change.

"Lover" is in the time signature of 3/4 and moves along fairly briskly. Count "1–2–3, 1–2–3," accenting the first beat in each measure.

Though all the chord names can be daunting, notice that each ii–V set in the verse is performed by sliding the same shapes down a half step.

Mairzy Doats *(page 104)*

A novelty song composed in 1943 by Drake, Hoffman, and Livingston, "Mairzy Doats" is a fun song full of misspelled (and mispronounced) words that seem to make nonsense. However, the bridge reveals all by not only correcting the spelling in the sheet music but also slowing down the melody and making the syllables much easier to understand. The Merry Macs had a #1 hit with the song in 1944, but it also resonated with American soldiers overseas, who supposedly used the nonsense portion of the lyrics to generate passwords. The song's also been featured in films, including *Radio Days* (1987), *The Cell* (2000), and in the TV show *Twin Peaks*, among others.

"Mairzy Doats" is played with a swing feel and moderate tempo. However, the quicker the tempo, the more jumbled the words sound in the verse, so feel free to try it a bit faster. In fact, it can be fun to speed up a bit with each repetition of the verse.

This song is in the key of C and makes use of several harmonic devices. There's a chromatic passing C#°7 chord to connect the C to Dm in the verse, and the bridge tonicizes the IV chord, F, with a ii–V progression of Gm–C7. (That's ii–V of IV.) Notice that the bridge continues on with a tonicization of G using Am–D7, which eventually leads back to C with Dm–G7.

For the bridge, the chords are often played sharply only once during the part where the lyrics are spelled out ("Mares eat oats and... ") to help make the joke clear.

Makin' Whoopee! (page 106)

A song first popularized by Eddie Cantor in the 1928 musical *Whoopee!,* "Makin' Whoopee" is a cautionary tale for men. It reveals that engaging in said whoopee, though seemingly enjoyable and harmless at first, can lead to the trappings of marriage, including washing dishes, washing baby clothes, and even — dare we say — sewing. The song's been given many successful treatments, notably by Ella Fitzgerald (1959), Doris Day and Danny Thomas (1952), Dr. John and Rickie Lee Jones (1989), and Rod Stewart and Elton John. Actress Michelle Pfeiffer also performed it for the 1989 film *The Fabulous Baker Boys,* starring brothers Jeff and Beau Bridges.

"Makin' Whoopee!," in the key of G, begins with a I–♯I°–ii–V progression (G–G♯°7–Am7–D7), in which the G♯°7 chord basically functions as a substitute for an E7 chord (see "High Hopes"). It's got a few other harmonic tricks up its sleeve too, most notably the ♭VI–V (E♭7–D7) move at the end of the phrase. This is another common chord progression that appears in numerous standards.

The bridge features an interesting progression of G♯°7–Am–Am7♭5–G, which you don't see every day.

The routing direction in this song is "D.S."— which stands for "Del Segno," (from the sign). It tells you to return to the "sign" (which looks like a slanted S with a line through it and two dots) and continue from there until you see the "To Coda" indication. In this song, the sign takes you to the beginning of the verse, which is extremely common.

Play this one with a swing feel as indicated and try strumming eighth notes. And watch out for the chromatic melody at the end of the verses!

Mr. Tambourine Man (page 108)

"Mr. Tambourine Man" is one of Bob Dylan's most beloved and enduring songs, although The Byrds also enjoyed a huge hit with the song when they covered it on their album of the same name — a seminal recording that many credit as the birth of folk rock. Originally released on Dylan's 1965 album *Bringing It All Back Home,* "Mr. Tambourine Man" contains verse upon verse of vivid imagery. The song has been covered by countless artists besides The Byrds throughout the years, including The Four Seasons, Judy Collins, William Shatner, The Barbarians, Alvin and the Chipmunks, and Bob Sinclair. No less than 13 cover versions were recorded in 1965 alone.

For all its lyrical splendor, "Mr. Tambourine Man" is a three-chord song using the I, IV, and V chords. In the key of A, this is A, D, and E. The simplicity of the harmony makes sense when you add the lyrics, because it would be difficult to let the words wash over you if the harmony was moving about unpredictably. Keep in mind that I've used a few different voicings of these chords (including E7 as well as E) to make things interesting on the uke.

Though first and second endings are most common, that won't do for a Bob Dylan song, who was known for his lengthy lyric sheets. Therefore, in this song you see first, second, third, and fourth endings in conjunction with the repeat signs. It still works the same way; it just means you play to that repeat sign two more times.

Although several voicings are presented for each chord here, don't worry too much about playing each one at the precise moment. The focus of a song like this is on the lyrics and melody; the accompaniment is only meant to support that. So feel free to play the whole song with only one voicing for each chord if you'd like, or mix and match them as you see fit.

Moonglow (page 114)

"Moonglow" (also known as "Moonglow and Love") was written in 1933 by Will Hudson and Irving Mills (music) and Eddie DeLange (lyrics). Originally recorded by Joe Venuti and His Orchestra in 1933, with versions by Ethel Waters and Benny Goodman and His Orchestra soon thereafter, the song has a melody line very similar to "Remember" by Irving Berlin. (Benny Goodman's version appears on the soundtrack for the 2004 Martin Scorsese film *The Aviator.*) The song has since become a jazz standard and has therefore been covered by numerous artists, including Art Tatum, Doris Day, Billie Holiday, Rod Stewart, and more.

Note that, although written in the key of G, "Moonglow" begins on the IV chord, Cmaj7. Though this isn't an uncommon occurrence, it confuses many, as some people make the mistake of thinking songs always start on the tonic chord. Aside from several standard secondary dominants, this song also features a ♭VII dominant chord, F7#11. This is an altered dominant chord, meaning that it contains either chord tones or extensions (the 11th in this case) that have been raised or lowered a half step.

Also notice that the bridge is essentially one long I–VI–II–V progression, with the V chord (D7) being proceeded by a ii chord (Am7).

"Moonglow" is played with a swing feel and usually at a fairly slow tempo (although Art Tatum and a few others have performed the song quite quickly). Note that many artists, when performing the song, treat the first 16 bars of the repeat as an instrumental interlude and begin singing again at the bridge. This type of variation is entirely up to the performer, especially since the lyrics don't change.

A steady, understated quarter-note strum works nicely for this tune on the uke. Most performers, however, do move to stop-time chords for the end of the phrases in the chorus and the outro (first encountered with the G chord in measure 7). Stop-time simply means to strike the chord once and then rest. This provides a nice bookmark to each phrase.

Now Is the Hour (Māori Farewell Song) (page 116)

"Now Is the Hour" is an old song with a colorful history, first published in Australia as an instrumental piano piece under the name "Swiss Cradle Song" in 1913. This version contained eight variations on the basic 16-bar theme. In 1915, Māori words were added, but it is unclear where they came from or who added them. The first English version is credited to Maewa Kaihau in 1920, though it wasn't copyrighted until 1928. The first recording of the song dates to 1927 when Ana Hato performed it with minor variations to the Kaihau lyrics. Since then, versions have been performed by Marty Robbins, Bing Crosby, Gale Storm, Frank Sinatra, and others. In 1915, the song was often performed as a farewell to Māori soldiers when shipping out for the first world war.

This is a slow 3/4 song played with a swing feel. The tempo is indicated at 92 beats per minute (bpm), but many performers often perform it even slower than that. Rhythmic liberty is often taken with the melody as well.

"Now Is the Hour" is in the key of F major, and aside from the V/V (read "five of five") secondary dominant chord, (see "Blue Hawaii" for more on secondary dominants) G7 in this case, you see a few more non-diatonic chords that merit mentioning. Namely, these include the minor iv chord, B♭m, and the augmented VI chord, D+. The minor iv chord is a wistful sounding chord that often resolves to the I chord and was favored heavily by The Beatles. The D+ chord in this case is still acting as a secondary dominant chord, but it's accommodating the B♭ melody note (the raised 5th of a D chord is A#, or B♭) temporarily as an augmented chord before sounding as a typical dominant chord on beat 3.

For this song, try strumming eighth notes with a flowing feel. Try to drag the strums slightly on the first beat of each measure to create a rolling, feathery attack. This song should sound as lush and pleasant as you can make it.

Ob-La-Di, Ob-La-Da (page 118)

Featured on the famous "White Album" (The Beatles), "Ob-La-Di, Ob-La-Da" is a reggae/ska-tinged McCartney composition that John Lennon admitted to hating upon first hearing. Eventually, after numerous failed attempts to record the song, Lennon played the chords on piano at a faster tempo, resulting in the song's winning formula. McCartney got the idea for the title and chorus line ("life goes on bra") from a Nigerian conga player named Jimmy Scott-Emaukpor, who used to frequently say them. Interestingly, the song wasn't released as a single in the U.S. (nor the UK) until 1976, where it reached #49, though it hit #1 in many other countries.

"Ob-La-Di, Ob-La-Da" is in the key of B♭ major and largely consists of the I, IV, and V chords (B♭, E♭, and F or F7). In the chorus, the iii chord (Dm) and vi chord (Gm) are added, which lends an interesting slant to the song's carefree message. Like many songs, the bridge (or middle eight) begins on the IV chord and ends on the V chord. This formula is present in thousands of songs.

Many of the melody phrases in this song begin off the beat (on the upbeat), meaning that the rhythm is *syncopated*. This syncopation is extremely important in maintaining the momentum of this song, so don't neglect this detail.

Seeing as this song has a reggae flavor, the upbeats (the "and" when counting eighth notes as "1 and 2 and 3 and 4 and") should be sharply accented to provide the proper groove. Ideally, you'd play this song with a bass player who would provide the bass line, allowing you to chop *only* the upbeats. However, even with no bass, this approach can still work. If this is the case, try to plant your strumming hand on the strings with a good bit of force for each downbeat, so you make a percussive tick on the beat in between strumming the upbeats with an upstroke.

Pearly Shells (Pupu `O `Ewa) (page 122)

"Pearly Shells (Pupu `O `Ewa)" is a Hawaiian song recorded by most notably Don Ho and Burl Ives. Based on a Hawaiian tune (with Hawaiian lyrics) called "Pupa A `O `Ewa," radio show host Webley Edwards wrote English lyrics to the tune with contributions from Leon Pober. In the song, the author casts an image of countless, beautiful pearly shells covering the shoreline and professes to his beloved that he loves her even more than "all the little pearly shells."

"Pearly Shells" is written in the key of B♭ major and uses predominantly the I (B♭), IV (E♭), and V (F or F7) chords of the key. However, there are other harmonies to spice things up, especially the iv chord (E♭m) and II chord (C7), which is a V/V secondary dominant (see "Blue Hawaii"). Notice that the iv chord (E♭m) occurs between the IV chord (E♭) and I chord (B♭), as is so often the case. Other notable harmonies include the iii chord (Dm) in the verse and the i°7 chord (B♭°7) in the bridge. The iii chord of a key is commonly used as a substitute for the I chord, as it shares two common tones: B♭ is spelled B♭–D–F, while Dm is spelled D–F–A.

Notice also that a chromatic *lower neighbor tone* is used in the melody during the bridge, as the A note (the 3rd of F7) is alternated with the G♯ a half step below. This lends a bluesy and playful tone that mirrors the lyrics, which speak in hyperbolic terms about the author having a kiss for his beloved to match every grain of sand on the beach.

The ⌢ symbol over the last note in the melody line is called a fermata. It indicates that the note and/or chord should be sustained for an extended period of time. It's commonly used for the last note of a song, but if used in the middle of the song, one of the performers will usually give a cue to indicate when to start playing in tempo once again.

This song should be played with a *bright* (quick) tempo and with a swing feel. Though most of the chords last for a measure or more, there are a few spots where they change on every beat. At this tempo, that's no easy task, so practice those spots slowly at first and make sure you're getting a clear chord on each beat.

Pocketful of Miracles *(page 111)*

"Pocketful of Miracles" is a Van Heusen/Cahn collaboration that was originally featured in the 1961 film of the same name, which starred Bette Davis, Glenn Ford, and Ann-Margret (in her film debut). The song was nominated for an Academy Award in the Best Song category. Several popular versions of the song were recorded, though Frank Sinatra's version is the most widely recognized. It's a light-spirited, optimistic song that speaks of finding miracles in life to counter the drudgery of the day-to-day.

Written in the key of G, "Pocketful of Miracles" is one of the most chordy songs in this book. There are secondary ii–V progressions (Bm7♭5–E7 in measure 4, Dm7–G7 at the start of the bridge), diminished chords all over the place, and lots of sixth and seventh chords. You'll definitely want to scan through the chords before tackling this one to brush up on any that aren't familiar to you. Many of them occur for only one beat, which is what makes this song especially tricky.

Notice that, at the start of the bridge, you tonicize the IV chord — an extremely common practice in standards. Also note that this song is a bit atypical in that, although it is an AABA format, the first two A sections last 12 measures each, the B section lasts eight measures (they don't call it the middle eight for nothin'!), and the final A section lasts 14 measures.

Although this melody features lots of quarter notes and few half notes, performers will rarely stick to what's written verbatim. Try listening to a few different versions of the song to hear different interpretations of the melody. The rhythm will most likely be altered the most, but melodic variations are quite common as well.

This song will sound nice with an eighth-note strum pattern (remember to swing the eighths), but feel free to mix it up with some quarter notes — especially during the phrase extension that contains the title line.

Puff the Magic Dragon (page 124)

Though it's hard to imagine it now, "Puff the Magic Dragon" was actually a huge pop hit in 1963 for Peter, Paul and Mary, reaching #2 on the Billboard chart. Peter Yarrow composed the music, but the lyrics were based on a poem by a 19-year old Cornell schoolmate named Leonard Lipton. After writing the poem on Yarrow's typewriter, he forgot about the poem and left it there. Years later, Yarrow tracked Lipton down to give him half the credit for the song, for which Lipton still receives publishing royalties.

Although urban legend has it that some of this song's lyrics — namely "Jackie Paper," "Puff," and "Dragon" — reference the use of marijuana, both Yarrow and Lipton (not to mention Paul Stookey and Mary Travers) have vehemently maintained that the song is simply about the loss of innocence and no drug references were ever implied whatsoever. This controversy was famously played upon in a scene from the 2000 film *Meet the Parents,* starring Robert De Niro and Ben Stiller.

"Puff the Magic Dragon" is in the key of A major and features almost exclusively diatonic chords — the only exception being B7, which is a secondary dominant (see "Blue Hawaii") that leads to the V chord, E7. The song is a bit unusual in that the verses and chorus use the same melody and music. In fact, the first verse is also the chorus of the song.

Note that at the end of the fourth chorus, the line "land called Honahlee" is extended to create a longer phrase that resolves on the tonic I chord. This is called a tag, and it's commonly found at the end of songs that feature a half cadence (resolving to the V chord) at the end of the form to properly resolve the phrase on the tonic.

For this song, try a strum pattern of "1–2–3 and–4 and, 1–2–3 and–4 and." In other words, you'll be strumming quarter notes on beats 1 and 2 and eighth notes on beats 3 and 4. Another pattern that works nicely is a quarter note on beat 1 and eighth notes on beats 2–4. Channel your inner child and resurrect the mighty Puff!

Raindrops Keep Fallin' on My Head (page 127)

Written for the 1969 film *Butch Cassidy and the Sundance Kid,* starring Paul Newman, "Raindrops Keep Fallin' on My Head" is a Hal David/Burt Bacharach collaboration. B.J. Thomas performed the original version and scored a #1 hit with the song in January of 1970. This version begins with a ukulele and features the instrument throughout the song. It's been featured in other films as well, including *Forrest Gump, Spy Hard* (which also includes a parody of the bicycle stunts performed in the original movie), *Spider Man 2,* and *Clerks II.* Other notable cover versions of the song include those by Perry Como, The Four Tops, The Flaming Lips, Ben Folds Five, and Barry Manilow.

This song is in the key of F major and begins with another common chord progression seen in hundreds of songs: I–Imaj7–I7–IV. In the key of F, this translates to F–Fmaj7–F7–B♭. Notice that a chromatic line of F–E–E♭–D is formed with this progression that lends a strong cohesion to a chord sequence that otherwise wouldn't seem to make much sense. A secondary ii–V progression of Am7–D7 occurs frequently as well and each time resolves to Gm7 as expected.

The Vsus4 chord, appearing here as C7sus4, is used prominently in the song as well and occurs at nearly every phrase end. Also briefly alluded to is a B7 chord for one beat in the bridge. Resolving to B♭ immediately afterward, this B7 chord is known in jazz language as a *tritone substitution.* A tritone is an interval of an augmented 4th or diminished 5th; it's three whole steps. In jazz, it's often used as a substitute for a dominant chord that's a tritone away. In this case, B7 is a tritone away from F7, so instead of just using F7 to lead to the IV chord, B♭, the tritone sub B7 is used to create a half-step move from B7 to B♭. It's definitely creates more tension than the standard F7, but it's acceptable because it goes by so quickly.

As is heard in the original version, an eighth-note strum pattern (remember that it's played with a swing feel) works well for this song. Notice however that the strum of beat 3 of each measure is played staccato. This type of detail lends a complexity and maturity to the music that can't be overstated. It's the little things that count!

San Francisco (Be Sure to Wear Some Flowers in Your Hair) (page 130)

Written by John Phillips (of The Mamas & the Papas) in promotion of the Monterey Pop Festival, "San Francisco (Be Sure to Wear Some Flowers in Your Hair)" was recorded by Scott McKenzie in 1967. A #1 hit in the UK and several other countries, it hit #4 in the U.S. and sold over seven million copies worldwide. Though he never enjoyed another hit of that magnitude, McKenzie did perform a new version with The Mamas & the Papas in 1986 and co-wrote the #1 Beach Boys hit "Kokomo" with Terry Melcher, Mike Love, and John Phillips in 1988.

The song was featured prominently in the film *Forrest Gump,* as well as *The Rock* and *Frantic.* It's considered a generational anthem and is thought to be partially responsible for thousands of young people relocating to San Francisco in the late 1960s.

 Arranged here in the key of C major, "San Francisco" is a brilliant study in how to make use of almost every diatonic chord in a key. (The only one not used is the vii°, which is by far the least common.) The verse begins with the very common progression of vi (Am)–IV (F)–I (C)–V (G), which, along with the variation of I–V–vi–IV, where the sequence simply begins two chords later, has fueled countless hits since the 1960s and still remains a staple in modern pop music (see "Hey, Soul Sister"). Notice that, to close out the first verse, the iii chord is used to provide a lift and refresh things.

The bridge contains the only non-diatonic chord in the song, when it surprisingly moves to the ♭VII chord (B♭) in proclamation of the generation's "new explanation."

After the bridge, songwriter John Phillips invokes another great songwriting strategy called reharmonization. Notice that, though the melody hasn't changed at the beginning of the third verse, the chords do. This is an often-overlooked technique that can breathe new life into previously-used material.

The song concludes with a *modulation* (change of key) up a whole step to D major and a restatement of a line from the second verse.

 For this song, use a strong eighth-note strum pattern and accent the backbeat (beats 2 and 4) by strumming extra hard. And if you've got any flowers lying around . . .

Satin Doll (page 136)

"Satin Doll" is a jazz standard written in 1953 by Duke Ellington and Billy Strayhorn. Johnny Mercer added lyrics to the song after it had already been an instrumental hit for several years. There are countless versions of this song, both with lyrics and instrumental, by artists such as Duke Ellington, Ella Fitzgerald, Nancy Wilson, Frank Sinatra, The Gaylords, Joe Pass, Oscar Peterson, Thelonious Monk, and many more.

"Satin Doll" is comprised of almost all ii–V changes strung together in different keys, the home key being C major. In the verse, we see the ii–V progression in four different keys alone: C (Dm7–G7), D (Em7–A7), G (Am7–D7), and G♭ (A♭m7–D♭7). Notice how melodic material is transposed from one set of ii–V changes to another — a common device in jazz composition.

The bridge continues this trend by opening with a ii–V in the key of F, the IV chord of the home key. The M.O. established in the verse is broken in the third measure of the bridge, however, when the Gm7–C7 progression actually resolves to F for the moment. The transposed melodic material is still present though in the Am7–D7 progression.

Because of the prevalence of ii–V changes in this song, it's often used by jazz soloists to practice their improvisational skills.

Jazz standards are often the subject of numerous arrangements, with added intros and/or outros, alternate chord changes, and a different order of material. So don't be surprised when you listen to versions of this song by different artists; they're not going to be the same. What's given here is a basic blueprint of the song's form. It can be manipulated or altered to suit the performer's or arranger's taste.

Try a quarter-note strum pattern for this song, allowing the eighth notes in the vocal line (either sung by you or played/sung by someone else) to provide the swing feel. In measures 5–6 (and subsequent repeats), try stop-time chords (see "Moonglow") to make it interesting.

Sing! (page 138)

"Sing!" is a novelty song from the 1975 Broadway Musical *A Chorus Line* — one of the most successful musicals in history. The song is "sung" from the standpoint of a dancer who never could sing. Nominated for 12 Tony Awards and winning nine of them, the musical tells the box-within-a-box story of 19 dancers auditioning for a part in the chorus line of an upcoming musical. A film of the same name directed by Richard Attenborough and starring Michael Douglas was released in 1985 to mixed critical reviews. Many critics and moviegoers felt that the idea was too difficult to translate to film.

It remains the longest-running musical originally produced in the U.S. and enjoyed a Broadway revival in 2006.

It's hard to perform this song solo, because the spoken parts are rattled off at quite a brisk pace, only to be answered by another performer who "sings" the final line of the sentences. The tempo is usually fairly brisk, which makes some of the one-beat chords a bit difficult. The song is in the key of E major and largely features the diatonic chords I, ii, IV, and V. Several of these are alternated with neighboring chords a half step away, as in measure 8, while others are approached with diminished chords a half step above, such as the G°7–F♯7 progression of measures 5–6.

The minor iv chord (Am7 and Am6) is featured toward the end of the second verse and leads to a I–♭VII–VI progression of E–D7–C♯7. Closer inspection, however, reveals that this D7 chord could actually be seen as a *tritone sub* (see "Raindrops Keep Fallin' on My Head") for G♯7, the secondary dominant of C♯7.

Leave any bit of seriousness at the door before approaching this song. It's supposed to be goofy, and you have to put on your actor hat to really sell it. Try to listen to the song to hear how the chords are sounded, as there are many stop-time sections.

(Sittin' On) The Dock of the Bay (page 133)

"(Sittin' On) The Dock of the Bay" is a celebrated classic co-written by guitarist Steve Cropper and legendary soul vocalist Otis Redding. While staying at a houseboat near San Francisco, Redding had scribbled out a few lines about the ships coming in and rolling back out again. Steve Cropper took what Redding had and finished most of the lyrics to complete the song. Unfortunately, the song would serve as a sort of swan song for Redding, who died just days after completing the recording. The song was released posthumously in 1967 and became a #1 — the first posthumous #1.

"Dock of the Bay" is in the key of G major and makes extensive use of non-resolving secondary dominants (see "Help Me Rhonda") in the verse. Both the B and A chords of the verse fit this description, as you may expect them to be followed by Em and D, respectively. Instead, B is followed by C, which is known as a *deceptive resolution,* while the A chord simply ends the phrase and is followed by the I chord, G, at the beginning of a new phrase.

The chorus contains yet another interesting non-resolving secondary dominant: the VI chord, E major. The A chord appears as well at the end of the section. It's at this point that you may realize that every chord in the song is a major chord, and that may shed a bit of light on the composition method. Sliding barre chords up and down on a guitar can result in such harmonies.

Although the chords shown here make up the backbone of the harmony, note that when performing this song many people will walk chords up and down chromatically during the verse. It is common that these chromatic notes are performed in the bass by a bass player or pianist.

For this song, try staccato chord chops on beats 2 and 4 to help simulate the snare drum. You can get a really nice effect by bringing your strumming hand down forcefully onto the strings as you strum to create a percussive "smack" for beats 2 and 4. This is really effective when playing as a solo performer.

Still the One (page 144)

Released in 1976, "Still the One" was a #5 hit for the soft rock group Orleans. The song was written by former member John Hall (with contributions by Johanna Hall) and featured on *Waking and Dreaming.* This was the band's second big hit, the first being "Dance with Me" a year earlier in 1975. Bill Anderson scored a country hit with the song in 1977, and the Republican campaigns of George W. Bush in 2004 and John McCain in 2008 used the song, much to the dismay of John Hall, who claimed that neither had secured permission to do so.

"Still the One" is a spirited number played with a shuffle feel. The routing here uses D.S. directions, codas, and numerous sets of multiple repeat endings, so be sure to scout things out before tearing into it.

This tune is in the key of E major and is largely a I–IV–V song with two notable exceptions throughout: the vi chord (C♯m7) and the II chord (F♯7), which classifies as a non-resolving secondary dominant (see "Help Me Rhonda").

The bridge moves to a *half-time feel,* meaning that the time is counted half as fast. This is a dynamic arrangement tactic that can inject a newfound energy into a song. It's often followed by a return to the normal feel, as is the case here. The ♭VII chord (D) makes an appearance in this section as the second non-diatonic chord in the song. This bridge section is reprised at the end (as is the half-time feel) to serve as the outro.

This is a great one to pull out at a campfire as a harmony song. Try strumming swung eighth notes throughout, with the exception of the half-time sections, where some quarter notes will help set the mood properly.

Supercalifragilisticexpialidocious (page 148)

A real word now found in dictionaries everywhere, "Supercalifragilisticexpialidocious" is also a song written by the Sherman brothers and first featured in the 1964 musical film *Mary Poppins.* In the film the song was performed by Julie Andrews and Dick Van Dyke. The phrase was coined by the brothers over a two-week period of double-talk and nonsense. Though it's been overanalyzed by many and claimed to mean many things, the film simply claims that it's "something to say when you have nothing to say." In 1997, the word was featured as the solution to a puzzle on *Wheel of Fortune.*

This tune is not very difficult to play, considering the fact that the chords usually last for several bars each, and there aren't that many of them in the whole song. The main harmonies are I (Cmaj7), V (G7), IV (F), and II (D7), although a few other chords are used as transitions to these, such as C♯°7 and C7. You'll notice too that, if you listen to the original version from *Mary Poppins,* the melody is definitely not taken literally.

This song is written in cut time. Therefore, it's counted brightly as "1–2, 1–2, "and so on.

This is a silly song and should be performed as such. Regarding the strum pattern, quarter notes will work fine, but with a tempo as bright as this, you'll most likely need to use alternating strokes for them.

Those Lazy-Hazy-Crazy Days of Summer (page 151)

The title track from Nat King Cole's 1963 album of the same name, "Those Lazy-Hazy-Crazy Days of Summer" is a light-spirited song that speaks of pretzels, beer, and girls in bikinis. Sounds like summer to me! The album featured arrangements by Ralph Carmichael, who also conducted the orchestra.

"Those Lazy-Hazy-Crazy Days of Summer" is in the key of B♭ (a common horn key) and features predominantly the tonic, II, and V chords, with many other chords sprinkled in between as transitions. The verse begins on the III chord, similar to the bridge of many songs, but the III–VI–II–V progression we expect is turned into a III (D7)–vi (Gm)–II (C7)–V (F7) progression with several short detours in between.

After the second chorus, the song modulates up a half step to the key of B major, repeating all the material in the new key. Note that a *tag* — a repetition of the final phrase one or more times — occurs at the very end of the song, which is a very common move in songs of this style.

This song is written in cut time and features a moderately bright tempo. Count "1–2, 1–2" with the 1 falling on "la" (from the word "lazy") and 2 falling on "ha" (from the word "hazy").

For this song, strum in quarter notes, keeping the strums on beats 2 and 4 nice and abrupt. This technique can make a song swing surprisingly well when performed with skill.

Time in a Bottle (page 156)

"Time in a Bottle" was originally featured on Jim Croce's 1972 album *You Don't Mess Around with Jim*. Three months after Croce's death in a plane crash in September of 1973, the song hit #1 on the Billboard charts in December of that year. Originally written for his son A.J., the song rose to fame after the success of his earlier hit single "Bad Bad Leroy Brown" (also from the same album). The song later appeared in compilations of Croce's love songs.

Numerous cover versions have been recorded through the years, including those by Glen Campbell, Jerry Reed, The Ventures, Floyd Cramer, Roger Whittaker, and more.

"Time in a Bottle" is in 3/4 meter, meaning that you count each measure as "1–2–3, 1–2–3," and so on. The first beat of each measure should be accented, with the second and third beats receiving equal emphasis.

Originally appearing in the key of D minor, "Time in a Bottle" is arranged here in the key of A minor for a better uke translation. It begins with a common chord sequence in which a minor chord occurs over a chromatically descending bass line. The same type of pattern is heard most famously in "Stairway to Heaven." In the verses, the harmony basically moves from the tonic (Am) to the iv (Dm) and finally to the V (E7), with passing chords in between.

For the bridge, you modulate to the parallel major, A major (see "The Fool on the Hill") and see a similar chord pattern in which you move from the tonic (A) to the IV (D) and then the V (E7) with passing chords in between. This is another common songwriting device — one that lends cohesion to a song while maintaining a renewed sense of interest.

A song like this really shines with a nice fingerpicking pattern. Try an eighth-note pattern where you roll through the string numbers as follows: 4–3–2–1–3–2, 4–3–2–1–3–2, and so on. Your right-hand fingers should be planted on the strings with the thumb on string 4, index on string 3, middle on string 2, and ring on string 1.

Tiny Bubbles (page 160)

"Tiny Bubbles," written and performed by Don Ho, appeared on the album of the same name in 1967 and reached #8 on the Billboard charts, while the album climbed to #57 on the strength of the single. Considered by many his signature song, it celebrates the tiny bubbles in wine and the feeling of euphoria they produce. Other notable versions of the song include those by Connie Francis, Lynn Anderson, and Kealoha Kono and His Orchestra.

"Tiny Bubbles" is in the key of D major, and the verses contain only the I (D), V (A7), and IV (G) chords arranged in a classic 16-bar form. The I chord moves to the V, which heads back to I, and then the IV chord kicks off the last half of the phrase, which is answered by a final I–V–I. This template is a common one in songs of all styles.

Another common move occurs in the bridge, with changes of IV–I–II (E7)–V, each lasting for two measures each to constitute the middle eight. For the third verse, the song modulates up a half step to E♭, with the verse section stated in the new key. The ending is extended by way of a tag (see "Those Lazy-Hazy-Crazy Days of Summer").

The "D.S." indication directs you to return to the sign — not the beginning of the song, as in "D.C." The sign is this song is located at the beginning of the verse. "Tiny Bubbles" is played at a moderate tempo with a swing feel.

A strum pattern of "1, 2–and, 3–and, 4–and" will work nicely with this song. Keep it light, bouncy — like bubbles in a glass of wine!

26 Miles (Santa Catalina) (page 163)

A #2 hit for The Four Preps in 1958, "26 Miles (Santa Catalina)" is a feel-good song praising the isle of Santa Catalina — the "island of romance." The song sold over a million copies and was featured on the *Ed Sullivan Show*. Written predominantly by the band's lead singer Bruce Belland while recovering from a broken ankle, the song is said to have influenced both Brian Wilson and Jimmy Buffett. Interestingly, Belland took up ukulele to pass the time after breaking his ankle, and it was on that instrument that he began writing what would eventually become this song.

"26 Miles (Santa Catalina)" is in the key of C and, until just before the bridge, consists of only four chords: I (C), vi (Am), ii (Dm7), and G7. This I–vi–ii–V progression is one of the most popular in history and is famously used in George Gershwin's "I Got Rhythm."

In the bridge, as is often the case, a dominant I chord (C7) leads way to the IV chord (F6). The rest of the bridge progression is extremely similar to the verse, only the beginning point of the phrase has shifted over two chords. A D7 secondary dominant (V/V) signals the end of the section by resolving to the V chord (G7), which continues on to resolve to the top of the verse in C.

In this song, the "D.C. al Coda" indication occurs at the end of a repeated section. Therefore, additional directions are included in the form of "2nd time," assuring you that you should play through the repeat before going back to the beginning of the song and playing until the "To Coda" indication.

The verse of this song is quite simple to play and sing at the same time, especially considering that the melody notes simply follow the roots of the chords throughout. Considering this, it's a nice song to practice with if you're not used to singing and playing simultaneously.

Walkin' After Midnight *(page 166)*

Written by Alan Block and Don Hecht originally for pop singer Kay Starr, "Walkin' After Midnight" went unused for some time after Starr's label rejected it. When Patsy Cline recorded it in 1957, it became the budding country star's first hit, reaching #2 on the Billboard country charts and #12 on the pop chart. The single, which tells the story of someone pacing the night streets in search of a beloved, sold over a million copies and is widely regarded as one of the all-time greatest country songs.

Written in the key of C, "Walkin' After Midnight" features fairly simple changes, mostly centered around the I (C), IV (F), and V (G) chords. However, several traits help lend a bluesy quality to the song. First of all, the IV chord appears prominently as a dominant chord (F7) in the verses, and the melody follows suit with a bold E♭ blue note. (E♭ is the ♭7th of F7.) Secondly, the verse wraps up with a jazzy progression of ♭VI (A♭7)–V (G7)–I, which is a common pattern in jazz and especially minor blues songs.

Par for the course, the bridge begins on the IV chord and moves back to the tonic via IV, I, IV, I–V changes. The final verse modulates up a half step to take the song out.

There are numerous blue notes in the melody for this song, and therefore there are plenty of courtesy accidentals to remind the performer of the key signature. Case in point is the E♭ note in measure 4, which is followed by an E in measure 5 with a courtesy natural sign.

The incomplete measure at the beginning of the song is called a pickup measure. You should begin by counting "1, 2, 3" and then come in on the "and" of beat 3.

Play this song with an eighth note strum pattern and swing the eighth notes all lazy-like. Picture Patsy strolling in the moonlight, gently swaying her hips back and forth.

What the World Needs Now Is Love *(page 172)*

A true David/Bacharach classic, "What the World Needs Now Is Love" was originally recorded by Jackie DeShannon in 1965 and featured on the album *This Is Jackie DeShannon*. The song was originally offered to Dionne Warwick, but she turned it down at the time. I'm sure Jackie didn't mind, as her version became a big hit, reaching #7 on the Billboard charts. It's also turned up in countless movies, including *Bob & Ted & Carol & Alice*, *Forrest Gump*, *Austin Powers: International Man of Mystery*, *My Best Friend's Wedding*, *Hot Shots!*, and *Happy Gilmore*. Countless covers exist as well by the likes of The Staple Singers, Luther Vandross, The Supremes, Wynonna Judd, Johnny Mathis, Aimee Mann, and Dionne Warwick.

"What the World Needs Now Is Love" is in 3/4 meter and is played with a swing feel. Accent the first beat of each measure with extra love.

This song is in the key of G major and begins on the iii chord, which is not all that common. All in all, there aren't too many non-diatonic chords in the tune, the most prominent being the B7 secondary dominant at the end of the chorus. This chord does resolve as expected to Em at the beginning of the verse. Toward the beginning of the verse, you have a secondary ii–V–I progression in C (Dm7–G7–Cmaj7), with the former two being non-diatonic. At the end of the verse is another secondary dominant, A7 (II), this time not resolving up a 4th as expected. Instead, it leads to the IV chord, which is another common chord sequence heard in countless songs such as "Yesterday" by the Beatles. The only other non-diatonic chord is heard at the coda: E7. This VI chord is another non-resolving secondary dominant that leads to the IV chord as well — a less common approach but still not unheard of.

Try strumming this one in swung eighth notes, but keep it light and airy. Try brushing through some of the strums for a slight harp effect to keep things interesting.

Yellow Bird (page 174)

"Yellow Bird" is derived from a 19th century Hawaiian song called "Choucoune" composed by Michel Mauleart Monton (music) and Oswald Durand (lyrics). In the 1950s, Alan and Marilyn Bergman composed new English lyrics for the song, resulting in "Yellow Bird." This song was first recorded in 1957 by the Norman Luboff Choir; Luboff was responsible for the song's calypso arrangement. The Mills Brothers enjoyed a minor hit (#70) with the song in 1959, but the most successful version was from the Arthur Lyman Group, who had a #4 hit in 1961. It's made TV appearances on *Here's Lucy* (1971) and *Murphy Brown* (1989) and continues to be a popular calypso song throughout the Caribbean.

"Yellow Bird" is written in the key of F major and features mostly the I, IV, and V chords in the chorus — the one exception being an F°7 chord that acts as a lower neighbor to the tonic chord, as it supports the B♮ in the melody. Beginning with the B♭6 chord, the melody begins to arpeggiate through the chords from low to high; its range is similar, but the notes are altered to fit each chord.

In the verse, the harmony moves to a I–ii–V progression, which, considering the fact that the IV chord was voiced as a B♭6, is very similar to the chords of the chorus. The chord sequence itself is different though, setting the two sections apart.

The tempo isn't all that quick on this song, but it's still notated in cut time. This is because the accents fall so squarely on beats 1 and 3 that it really feels like only two beats per measure. Listen to a few versions of the song to hear how this feels.

The chords here are not difficult — the only full barre chord is B♭6 — and, with the exception of the F°7, they don't change quickly. So you can take your time with the strums and really feather the strings at times for a lush effect.

Yellow Submarine (page 169)

"Yellow Submarine" is a McCartney composition credited to Lennon/McCartney and sung by Ringo. Originally appearing on the *Revolver* album in 1966, the single (backed with "Eleanor Rigby") hit #2 in the U.S. and #1 in the UK. However, the song regained new life two years later with the release of the animated film of the same name. Telling the tale of underwater dwellings in a yellow submarine, the song was intended to be a children's song. Today, it's included in countless children's song compilations and is a favorite in many countries.

"Yellow Submarine" is arranged here in the key of G major and begins on the V chord, which is a bit unusual. All the chords in this song are diatonic to the key, and every diatonic chord in the key (save for the vii°) is used at some point. The harmonic rhythm throughout the verse is a lopsided one, with the chords arranged in beats of 3 and then 1. The chords in the chorus return to a more standard rhythm.

For the verse, try strumming each chord only once, as a similar method is used on the original recording. Once the chorus kicks in, get everyone's head bobbing with a swung eighth-note strum pattern.

Notice that the segno (𝄋) is a bit more hidden in this song, so be sure to mark it before you dive down into the sea of green.

You Are My Sunshine (page 176)

First recorded in 1939 by The Pine Ridge Boys and shortly thereafter by The Rice Brothers Gang and by Jimmie Davis in 1939 and 1940, respectively, "You Are My Sunshine" is one of the country's most popular songs, known to old and young alike. The authorship of the song is the subject of some debate, as Jimmie Davis and Charles Mitchell are credited, though Davis has admitted that he purchased the song rights from Paul Rice and listed himself as the songwriter. This practice was much more common before WWII. Hundreds of cover versions exist of the song, including ones by Bing Crosby, Gene Autry, Tony Sheridan, Billy Haley & His Comets, Bob Dylan, Johnny Cash, Brian Wilson, and Aretha Franklin, among many more. It's become a popular children's song, although the chorus is usually the only lyric sung in such instances.

Written in the key of D major, "You Are My Sunshine" is a three-chord song, using only the I, IV, and V chords of the key. The tonic dominant chord (D7) is used as well as a secondary dominant leading to the IV chord at times. Though harmonically simple, the melody is quite nice and memorable. Containing mostly quarter notes and half notes (and usually performed in this manner), this makes a good uptempo song to begin with if singing and playing together is new to you.

This song is played with a swing feel and should be brisk enough to almost be felt in cut time.

For "You Are My Sunshine," try strumming in a pattern of "1, 2, 3–and, 4–and." In other words, you'll play quarter notes on beats 1 and 2 and eighth notes on beats 3 and 4. This is a great pattern to use on uptempo shuffle songs such as this. Try to accent beat 2 a little more than the rest.

Mairzy Doats

Words and Music by Milton Drake, Al Hoffman and Jerry Livingston

lit - tle bit jum - bled and jiv – ey, sing "Mares eat oats and

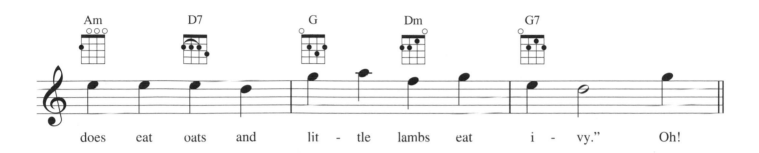

does eat oats and lit – tle lambs eat i – vy." Oh!

Outro-Verse

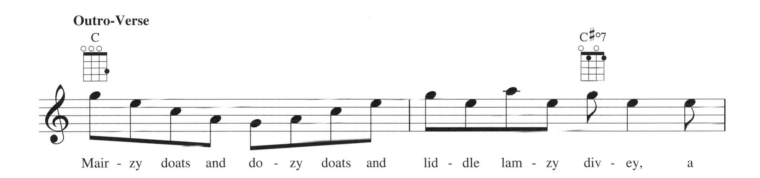

Mair - zy doats and do - zy doats and lid - dle lam - zy div - ey, a

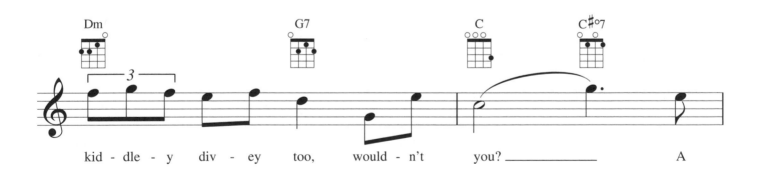

kid - dle - y div – ey too, would - n't you? _____ A

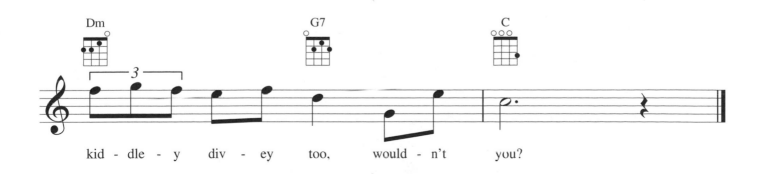

kid - dle - y div – ey too, would - n't you?

Makin' Whoopee!

from WHOOPEE!
Lyrics by Gus Kahn
Music by Walter Donaldson

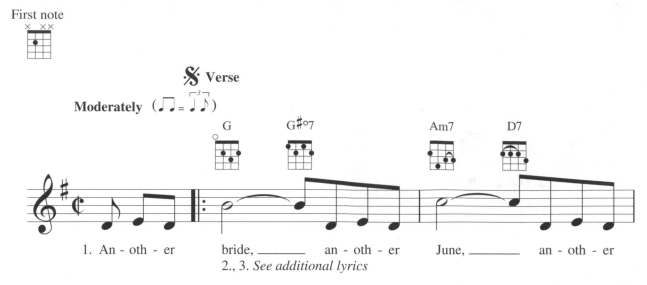

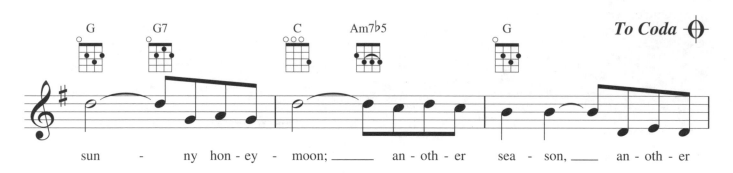

sun - ny hon-ey - moon; _____ an - oth - er sea - son, _____ an - oth - er

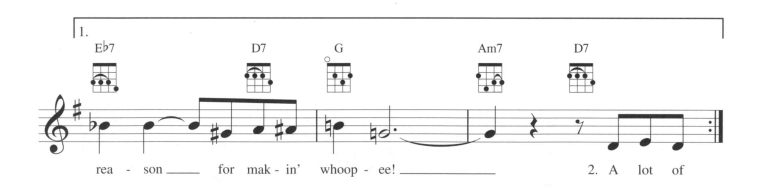

rea - son _____ for mak - in' whoop - ee! _____ 2. A lot of

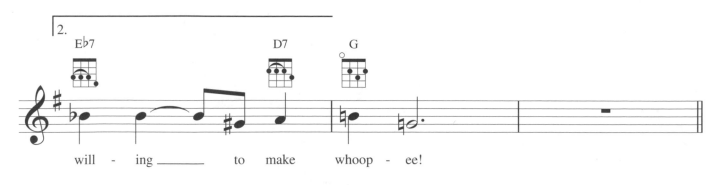

will - ing _____ to make whoop - ee!

Bridge

Pic - ture a lit - tle love - nest, down where the ros - es

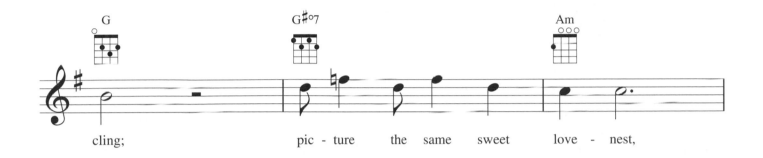

cling; pic - ture the same sweet love - nest,

D.S. al Coda

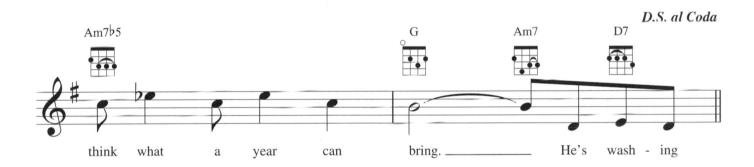

think what a year can bring. _____ He's wash - ing

✛ **Coda**

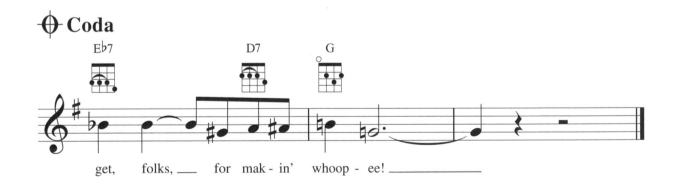

get, folks, ___ for mak - in' whoop - ee! _____

Additional Lyrics

2. A lot of shoes, a lot of rice,
   The groom is nervous; he answers twice.
   It's really killing that he's so willing
   To make whoopee!

3. He's washing dishes and baby clothes.
   He's so ambitious; he even sews.
   But don't forget, folks, that's what you get, folks,
   For makin' whoopee!

Mr. Tambourine Man

Words and Music by Bob Dylan

an - cient emp - ty street's too dead for dream - in'. _____

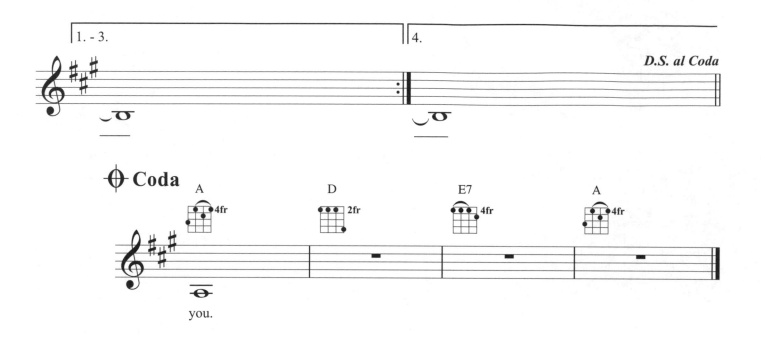

|1. - 3. |4.

D.S. al Coda

⊕ Coda

you.

Additional Lyrics

2. Take me on a trip upon your magic swirlin' ship
    My senses have been stripped, my hands can't feel to grip
    My toes too numb to step, wait only for my boot heels
    To be wanderin'
    I'm ready to go anywhere, I'm ready for to fade
    Into my own parade, cast your dancin' spell my way
    I promise to go under it.

3. Though you might hear laughin' spinnin' swingin' madly across the sun
    It's not aimed at anyone, it's just escapin' on the run
    And but for the sky there are no fences facin'
    And if you hear vague traces of skippin' reels of rhyme
    To your tambourine in time, it's just a ragged clown behind
    I wouldn't pay it any mind, it's just a shadow you're
    Seein' that he's chasin'.

4. Then take me disappearin' through the smoke rings of my mind
    Down the foggy ruins of time, far past the frozen leaves
    The haunted, frightened trees out to the windy beach
    Far from the twisted reach of crazy sorrow
    Yes, to dance beneath the diamond sky with one hand wavin' free
    Silhouetted by the sea, circled by the circus sands
    With all memory and fate driven deep beneath the waves
    Let me forget about today until tomorrow.

Pocketful of Miracles

Words by Sammy Cahn
Music by Janes Van Heusen

Moonglow

Words and Music by Will Hudson, Eddie De Lange and Irving Mills

Now Is the Hour
(Māori Farewell Song)

Words and Music by Clement Scott, Maewa Kaithau and Dorothy Stewart

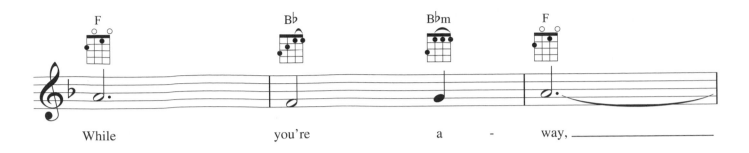

While you're a - way, _____

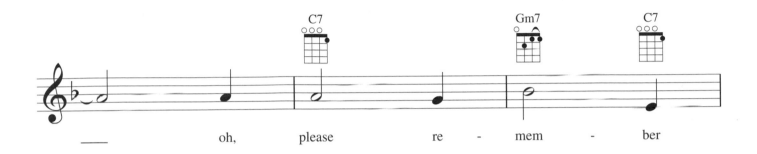

___ oh, please re - mem - ber

me. _____ When

you re - turn, you'll find me

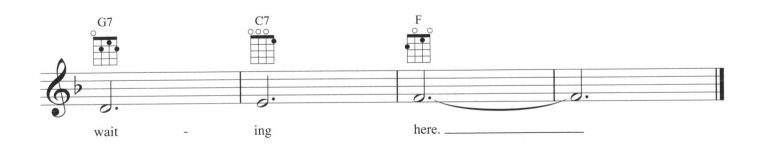

wait - ing here. _____

Ob-La-Di, Ob-La-Da

Words and Music by John Lennon and Paul McCartney

First note

Intro
Moderately ♩ = 114

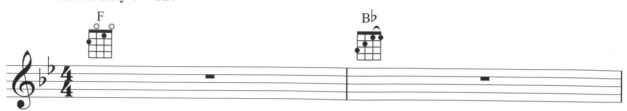

Verse

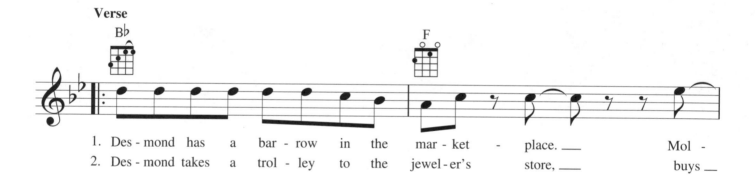

1. Des - mond has a bar - row in the mar - ket - place. ___ Mol -
2. Des - mond takes a trol - ley to the jewel - er's store, ___ buys

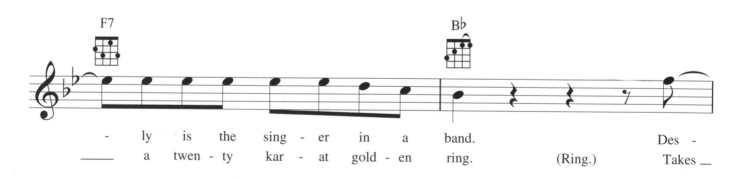

- ly is the sing - er in a band. Des -
___ a twen - ty kar - at gold - en ring. (Ring.) Takes

- mond says to Mol - ly, "Girl, I like your face," ___ and Mol - ly
___ it back to Mol - ly wait - ing at the door, ___ and as he

says this as she takes him by the hand. ___ } (Sing.) Ob - la - di, ___
gives it to her she beg - ins to sing. ___

Chorus

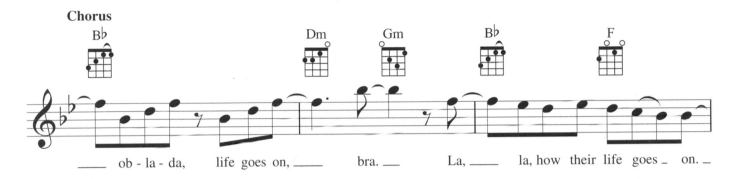

___ ob - la - da, life goes on, ___ bra. ___ La, ___ la, how their life goes _ on. ___

___ Ob - la - di, ob - la - da, life goes on, ___ bra. ___ La, ___

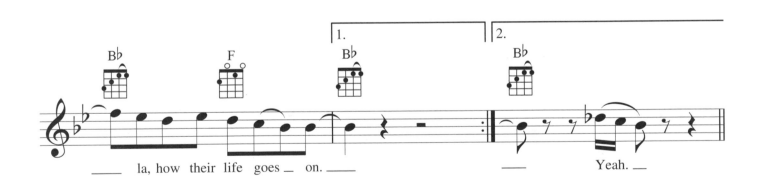

___ la, how their life goes _ on. ___ Yeah. ___

Bridge

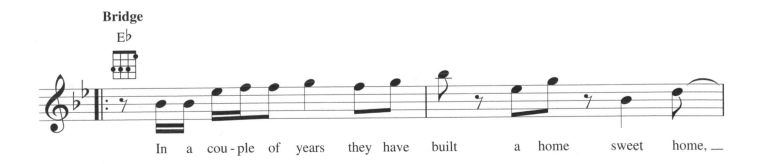

In a cou - ple of years they have built a home sweet home, ___

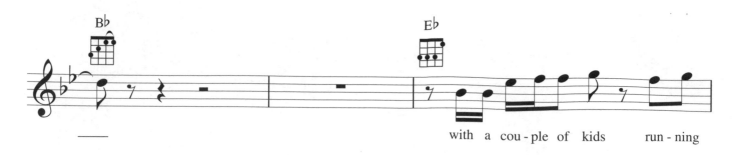

with a cou - ple of kids   run - ning

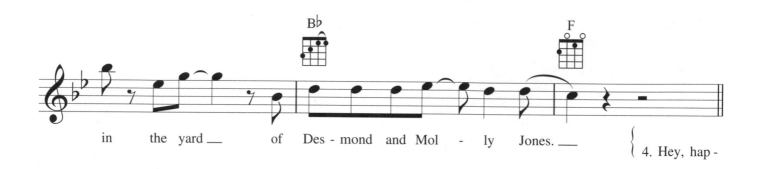

in   the yard ___   of Des - mond and Mol - ly Jones. ___

{ 4. Hey, hap -

Verse

3. Hap - py ev - er af - ter in the mar - ket - place, ___   Des -
    - py ev - er af - ter in the mar - ket - place, ___   Mol -

- mond lets the child - ren lend a hand.   Mol -
- ly lets the child - ren lend a hand.   Des -

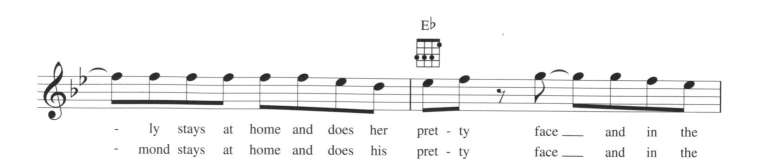

- ly stays at home and does her pret - ty   face ___ and in the
- mond stays at home and does his pret - ty   face ___ and in the

eve - ning she still sings it with the band. ___ Yes, ___ } ob - la - di,
eve - ning she's a sing - er with the band. ___ Yeah, ___

Chorus

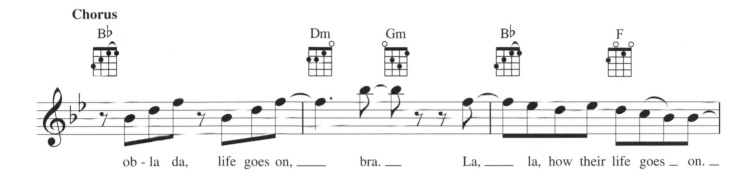

ob - la da, life goes on, ___ bra. ___ La, ___ la, how their life goes _ on. _

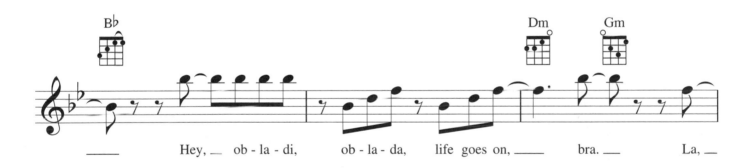

___ Hey, _ ob - la - di, ob - la - da, life goes on, ___ bra. ___ La, _

___ la, how their life goes _ on. ___ Well, if you

Outro

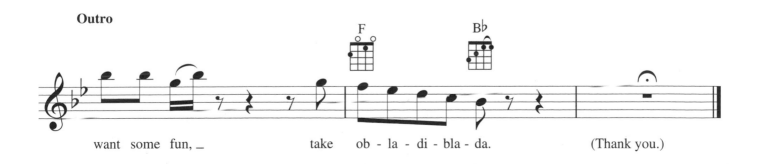

want some fun, _ take ob - la - di - bla - da. (Thank you.)

Pearly Shells
(Pupu `O `Ewa)
Words and Music by Webley Edwards and Leon Pober

Puff the Magic Dragon

Words and Music by Lenny Lipton and Peter Yarrow

First note

Intro
Brightly

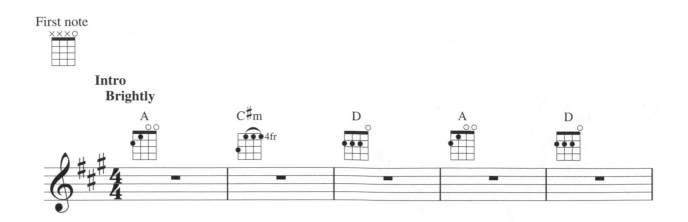

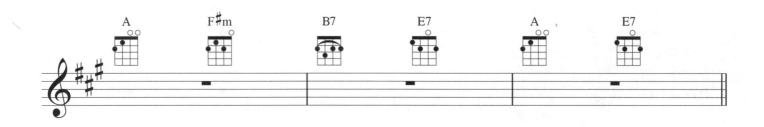

Verse

1. Puff,   the mag - ic   dra - gon,   lived by ____ the
   geth - er   they would   trav - el   on a   boat with   bil - lowed

3., 4. *See additional lyrics*
       (skip Chorus after 3rd Verse)

sea   and   frol - icked in ____ the   au - tumn mist ____ in a
sail;   and   Jack - ie   kept a   look - out perched __ on

Additional Lyrics

3. A dragon lives forever, but not so little boys.
   Painted wings and giant rings make way for other toys.
   One gray night it happened, Jackie Paper came no more,
   And Puff that mighty dragon, he ceased his fearless roar. (to Verse 4)

4. His head was bent in sorrow, green tears fell like rain.
   Puff no longer went to play along the Cherry Lane.
   Without his lifelong friend, Puff could not be brave,
   So Puff that mighty dragon sadly slipped into his cave. Oh!

Raindrops Keep Fallin' on My Head

Lyric by Hal David
Music by Burt Bacharach

the blues ___ they send ___ to meet ___ me won't de-feat ___

___ me. It won't be long ___ till hap-pi-ness ___ steps up ___

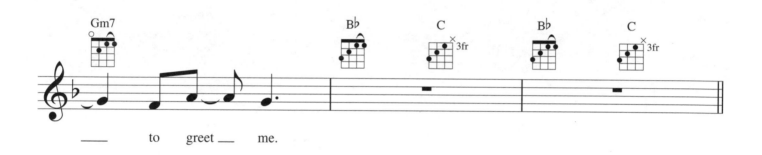

___ to greet ___ me.

Verse

3., 4. Rain-drops keep fall-in' on my head, but

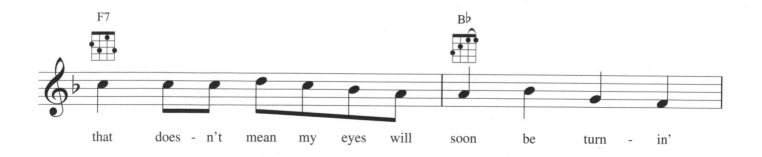

that does-n't mean my eyes will soon be turn-in'

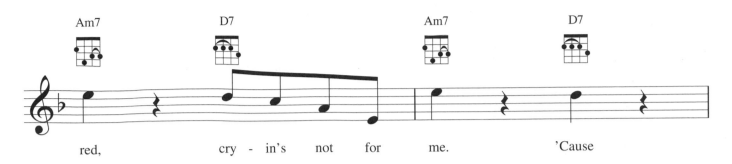

red, cry - in's not for me. 'Cause

I'm nev - er gon - na stop the rain by com - plain - in'. Be - cause I'm

To Coda ⊕   **Bridge**

free. _____   Noth - in's wor - ry - in'   me. *Instrumental*

D.S. al Coda

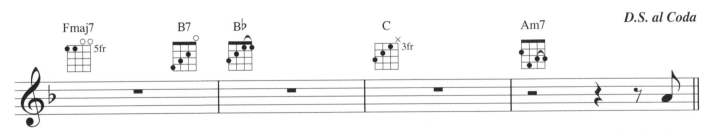

Instrumental ends It

⊕ **Coda**

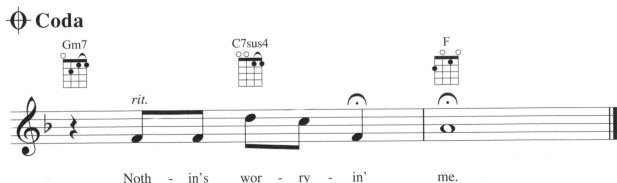

Noth - in's wor - ry - in'   me.

San Francisco

(Be Sure to Wear Some Flowers in Your Hair)

Words and Music by John Phillips

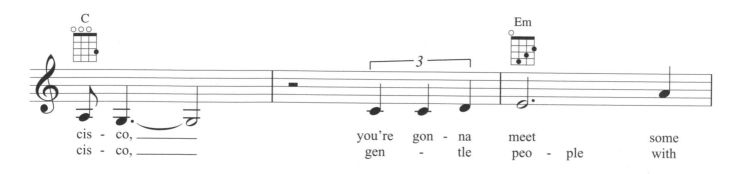

gen - tle peo - ple there. _____
flow - ers in ___ their hair. _____

Bridge

All a-cross the na - tion, ___ such a strange vi - bra - tion: _____

___ peo ple in mo - tion. ___ There's a whole gen - er - a-

- tion _____ with a new ex - pla - na - tion. _____

___ Peo-ple in mo - tion. ___ Peo-ple in mo - tion.

Verse

3. For those who come to San Fran - cis- co, _____ be sure to

wear some flow-ers in your hair. _____ If you come _____ to

San Fran - cis - co _____ sum - mer - time will

Outro

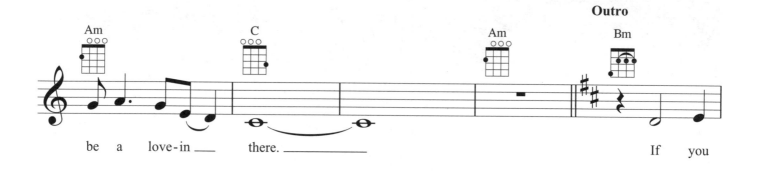

be a love-in _____ there. _____ If you

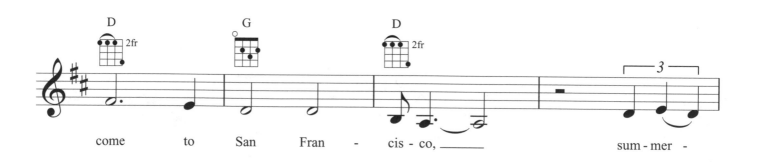

come to San Fran - cis - co, _____ sum - mer -

time _____ will be a love-in _____ there. _____

(Sittin' On) The Dock of the Bay

Words and Music by Steve Cropper and Otis Redding

1. Sit - tin' in the morn - ing sun, ___
2., 3. *See additional lyrics*

I'll be sit - tin' when the eve - ning comes. ___

Watch - ing the ships roll in, ___

then I watch 'em roll a - way a - gain. ___

Chorus

Yeah, ___ I'm sit - tin' on the
So, ___ I'm just gon' sit on the } dock of the bay, ___
Now, ___ I'm just gon' sit on the

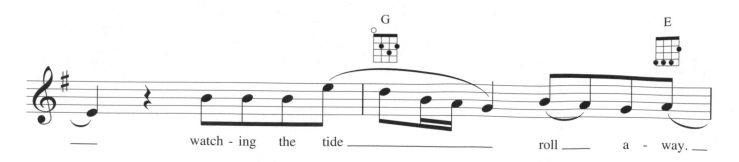

watch - ing the tide _____ roll ____ a - way. ___

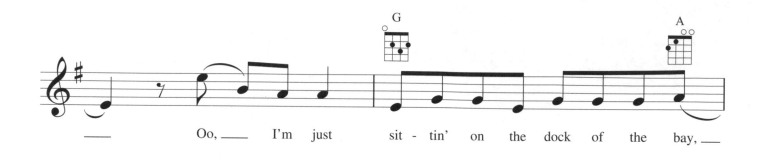

___ Oo, ____ I'm just sit - tin' on the dock of the bay, ___

To Coda

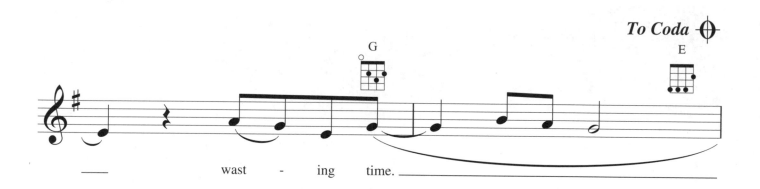

___ wast - ing time. _____

1.   2.   **Bridge**

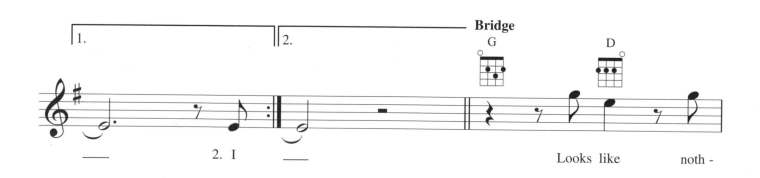

___   2. I ___   Looks like noth -

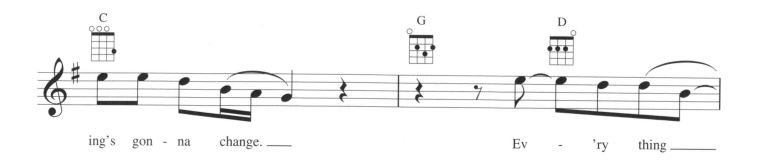

ing's gon - na change. ____   Ev - 'ry thing _____

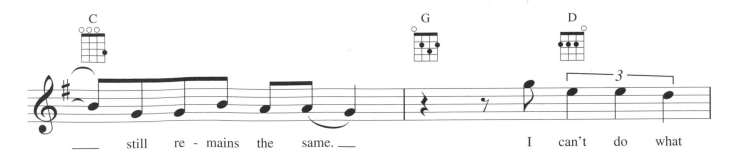

still re - mains the same. ___ I can't do what

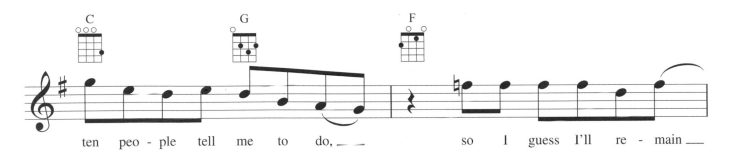

ten peo - ple tell me to do, ___ so I guess I'll re - main ___

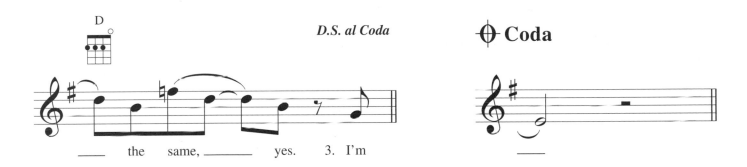

D.S. al Coda   ⊕ **Coda**

___ the same, ___ yes.   3. I'm   ___

Outro   *Repeat and fade*

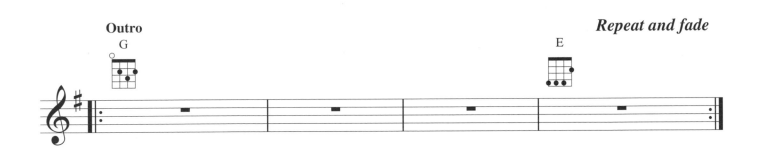

Additional Lyrics

2. I left my home in Georgia,
   Headed for the Frisco bay.
   I have nothin' to live for,
   Look like nothin's gonna come my way.

3. Sittin' here restin' my bones,
   And this loneliness won't leave me alone.
   Two thousand miles I roam,
   Just to make this dock my home.

Satin Doll

from SOPHISTICATED LADIES
Words by Johnny Mercer and Billy Strayhorn
Music by Duke Ellington

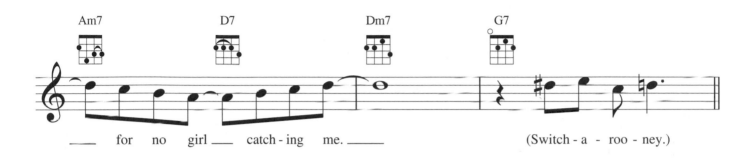

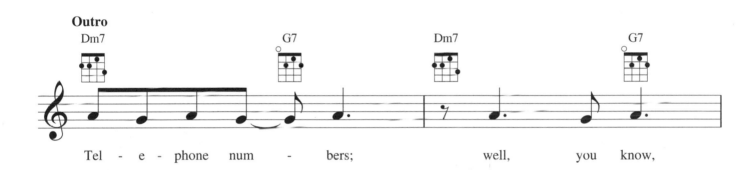

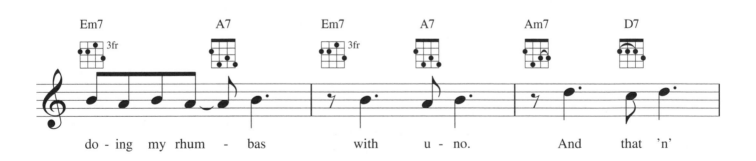

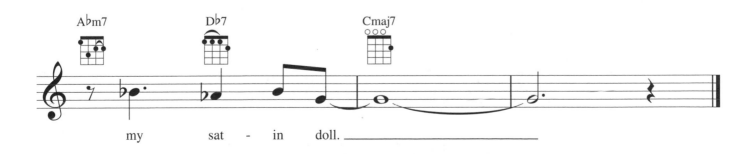

Sing!

from A CHORUS LINE
Music by Marvin Hamlisch
Lyric by Edward Kleban

First note

Verse
Moderately fast

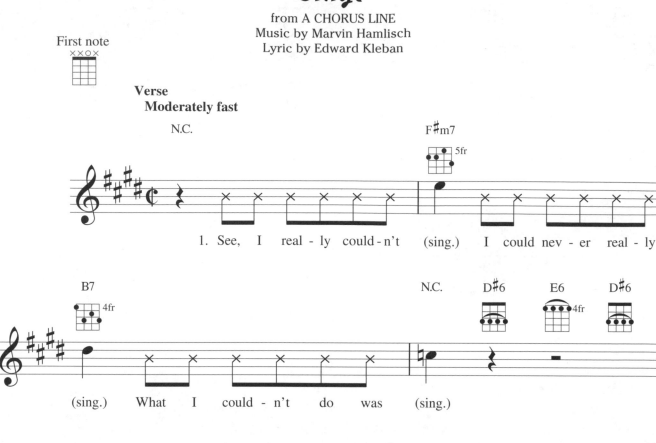

1. See, I real-ly could-n't (sing.) I could nev-er real-ly

(sing.) What I could-n't do was (sing.)

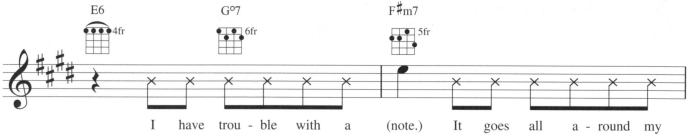

I have trou-ble with a (note.) It goes all a-round my

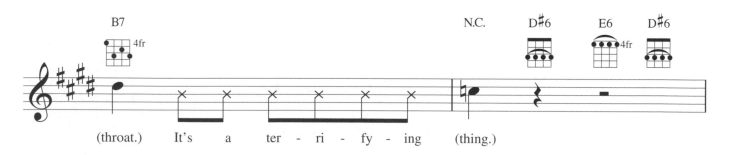

(throat.) It's a ter-ri-fy-ing (thing.)

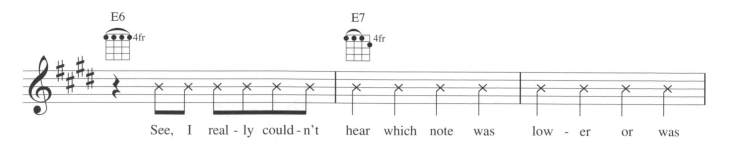

See, I real-ly could-n't hear which note was low-er or was

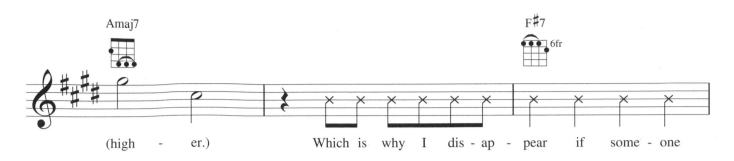

(high - er.) Which is why I dis - ap - pear if some - one

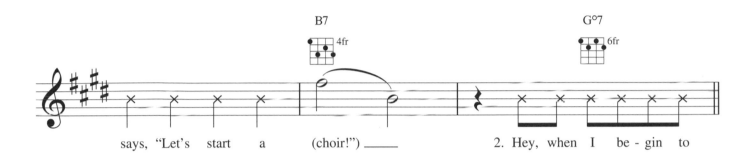

says, "Let's start a (choir!") _____ 2. Hey, when I be - gin to

Verse

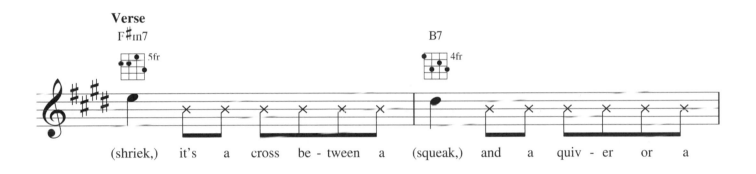

(shriek,) it's a cross be - tween a (squeak,) and a quiv - er or a

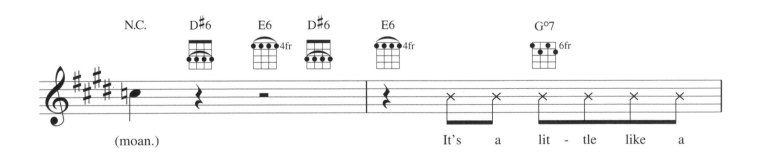

(moan.) It's a lit - tle like a

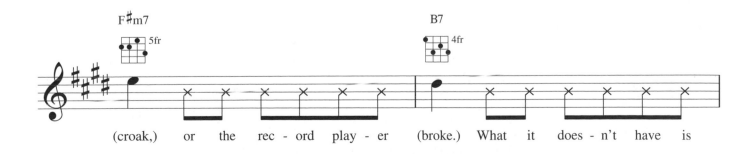

(croak,) or the rec - ord play - er (broke.) What it does - n't have is

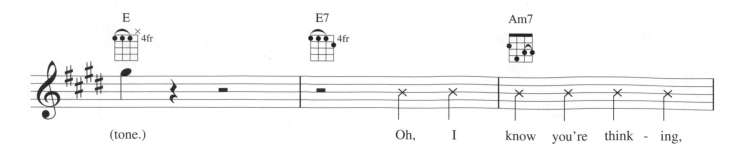

(tone.)   Oh,   I   know   you're   think - ing,

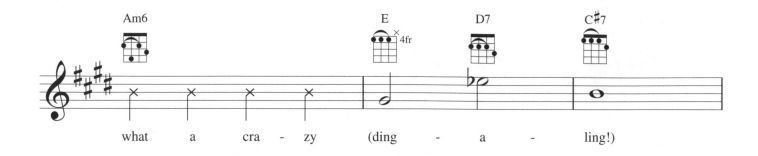

what   a   cra - zy   (ding - a - ling!)

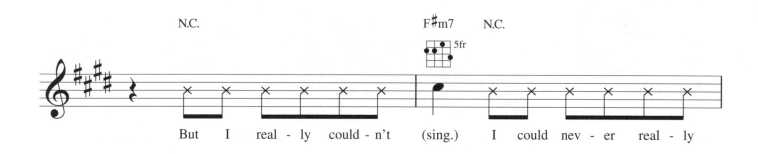

But   I   real - ly   could - n't   (sing.)   I   could   nev - er   real - ly

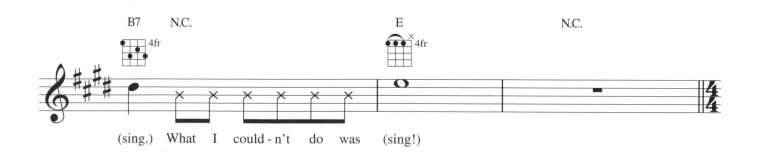

(sing.)   What   I   could - n't   do   was   (sing!)

Bridge

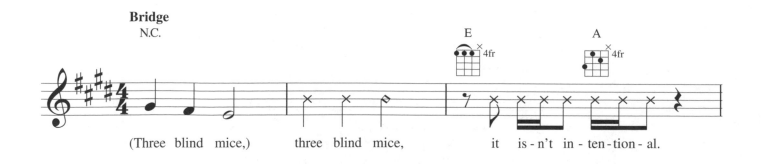

(Three   blind   mice,)   three   blind   mice,   it   is - n't   in - ten - tion - al.

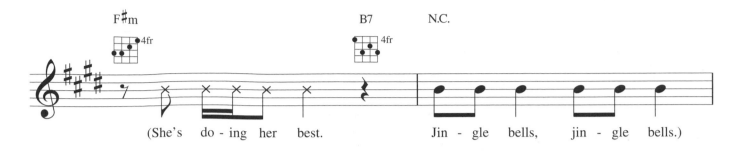

(She's do - ing her best. Jin - gle bells, jin - gle bells.)

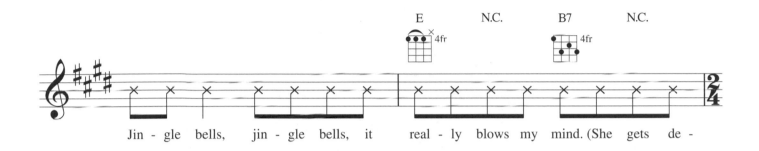

Jin - gle bells, jin - gle bells, it real - ly blows my mind. (She gets de -

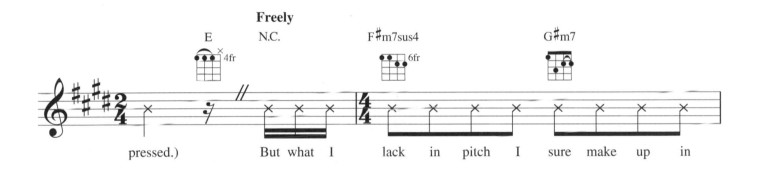

Freely

pressed.) But what I lack in pitch I sure make up in

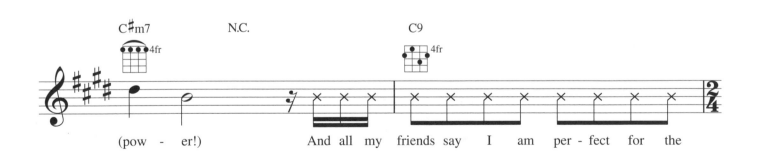

(pow - er!) And all my friends say I am per - fect for the

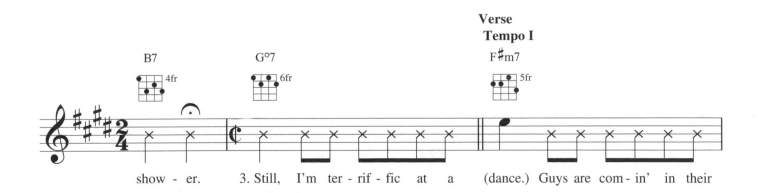

Verse
Tempo I

show - er. 3. Still, I'm ter - rif - fic at a (dance.) Guys are com - in' in their

Still the One

Words and Music by John Hall and Johanna Hall

Bridge
Half-time feel

End half-time feel

Chorus

* 2nd time, N.C., next 6 meas.

Supercalifragilisticexpealidocious

from Walt Disney's MARY POPPINS
Words and Music by Richard M. Sherman and Robert B. Sherman

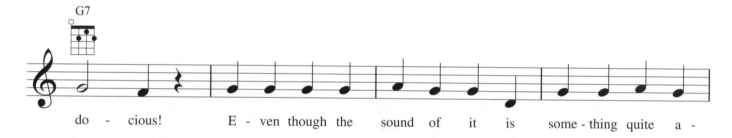

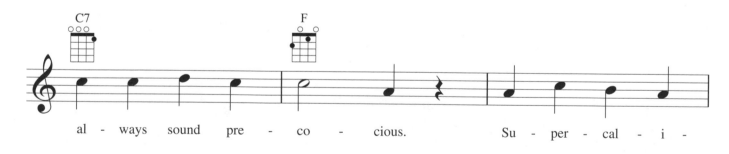

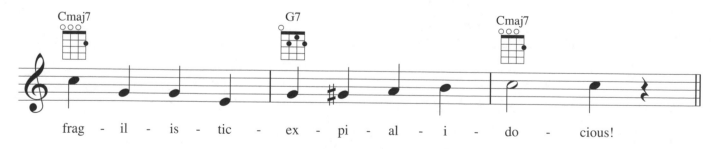

Those Lazy-Hazy-Crazy Days of Summer

Words by Charles Tobias
Music by Hans Carste

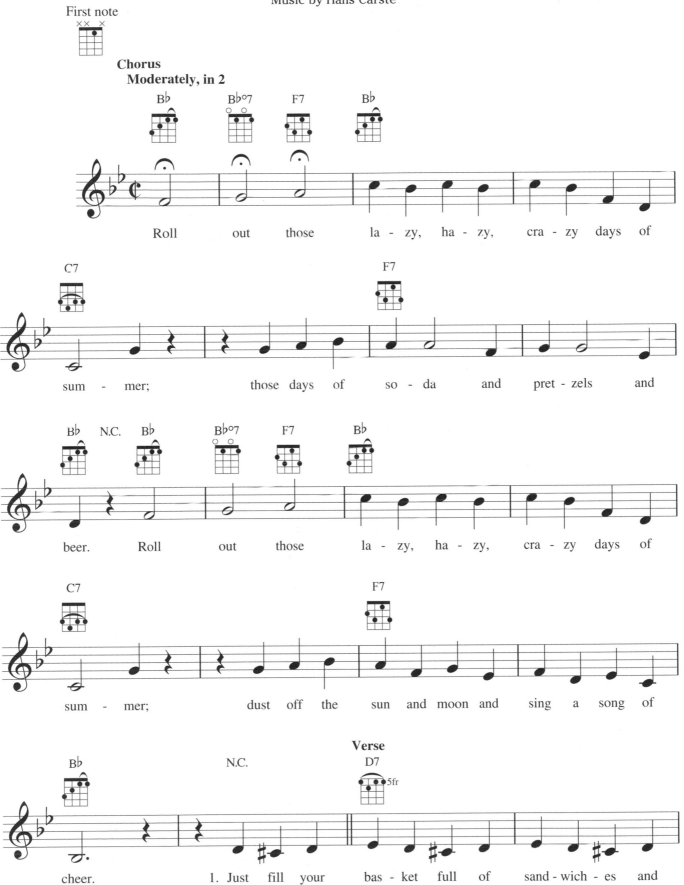

ween - ies,   then lock the house up,   now you're

Gm   C7   Gm7   B7

set.   And on the beach, you'll see the girls in their bi -

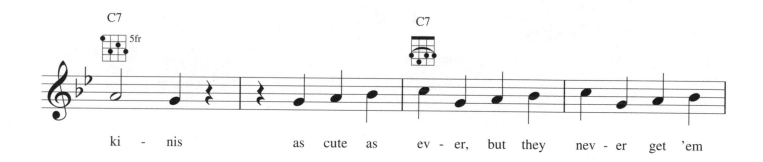

C7   C7

ki - nis   as cute as ev - er, but they nev - er get 'em

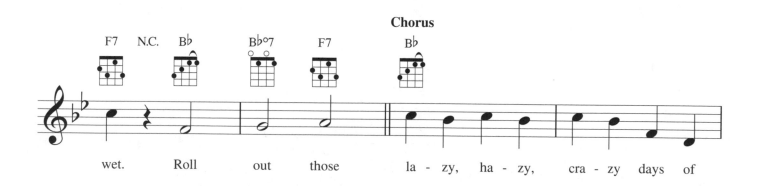

Chorus

F7 N.C. Bb   Bb°7   F7   Bb

wet.   Roll out those   la - zy, ha - zy, cra - zy days of

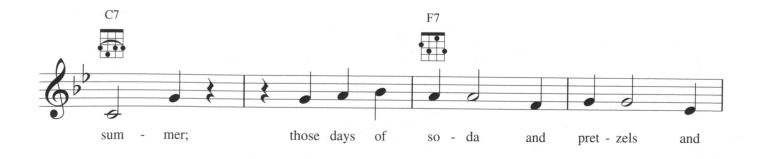

C7   F7

sum - mer;   those days of so - da and pret - zels and

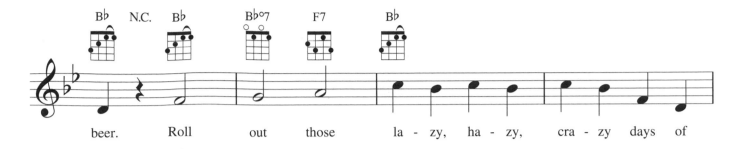

beer. Roll out those la - zy, ha - zy, cra - zy days of

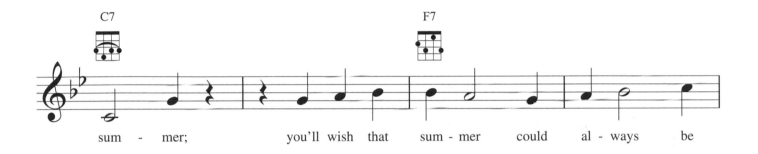

sum - mer; you'll wish that sum - mer could al - ways be

Chorus

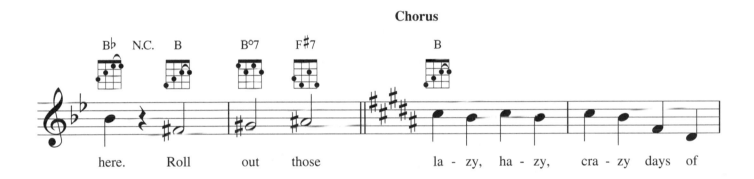

here. Roll out those la - zy, ha - zy, cra - zy days of

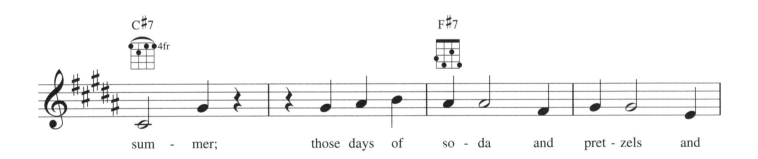

sum - mer; those days of so - da and pret - zels and

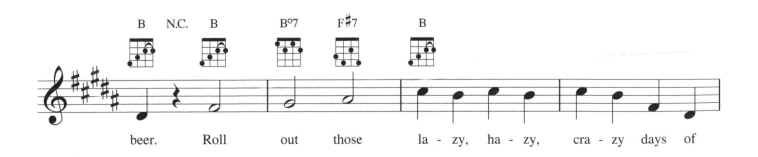

beer. Roll out those la - zy, ha - zy, cra - zy days of

sum - mer; dust off the sun and moon and sing a song of

Verse

cheer. 2. Don't have to tell a girl or fel - la 'bout a

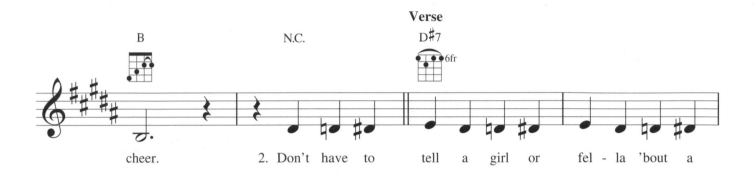

drive in or some ro - man - tic mov - ie

scene. Why, from the mo - ment that those lov - ers start ar -

riv - in', you'll see more kiss - ing in the cars than on the

Time in a Bottle

Words and Music by Jim Croce

First note

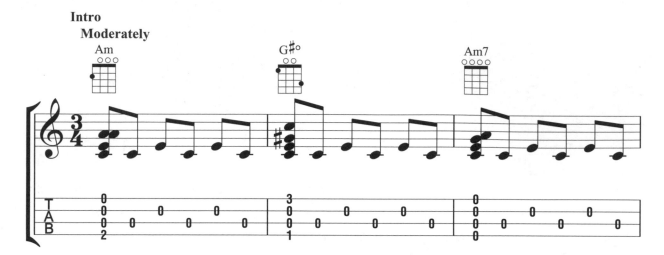

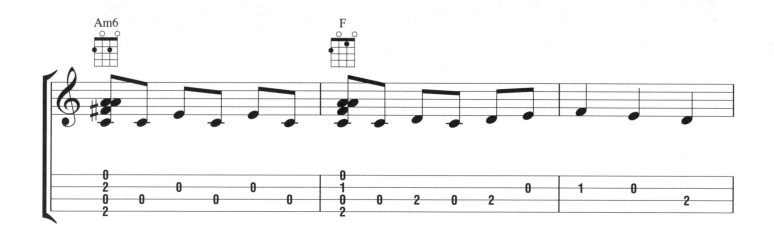

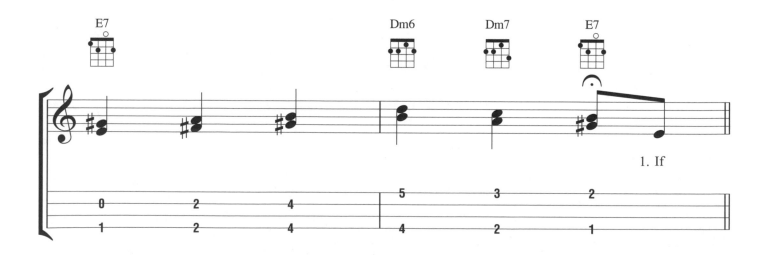

Verse

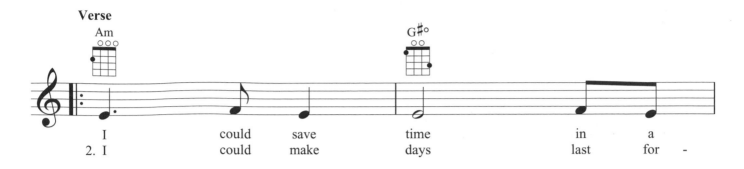

I   could   save   time   in   a
2. I   could   make   days   last   for -

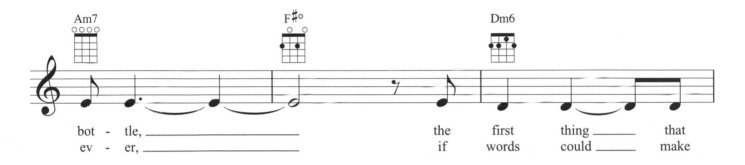

bot - tle, _____   the   first   thing _____ that
ev - er, _____   if   words   could _____ make

I'd   like   to   do _____   is   to   save   ev -'ry   day   'til e -
wish - es   come   true, _____   I'd   save   ev -'ry   day   like   a

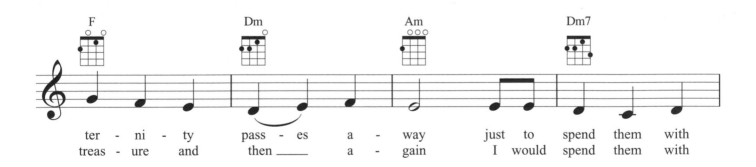

ter - ni - ty   pass - es   a - way   just   to   spend   them   with
treas - ure   and   then ____ a - gain   I   would   spend   them   with

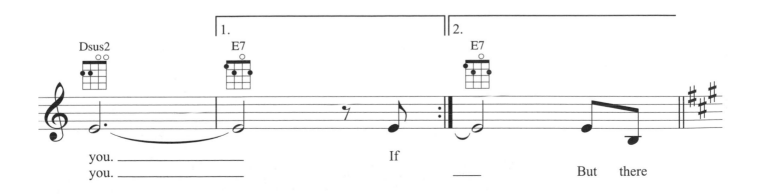

you. _____
you. _____   If

                      ____   But   there

nev - er seems ___ to be e - nough time to do the things ___ you

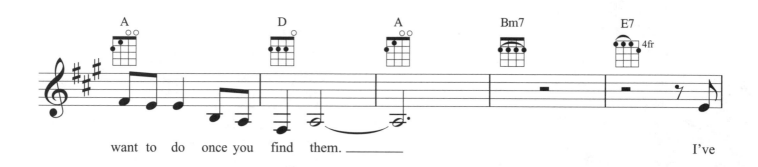

want to do once you find them. _____ I've

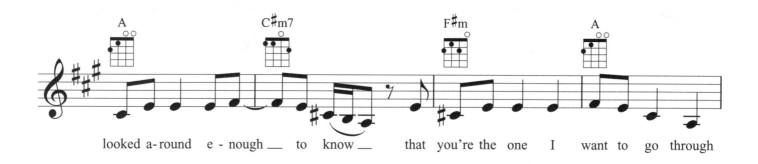

looked a-round e - nough ___ to know ___ that you're the one I want to go through

To Coda

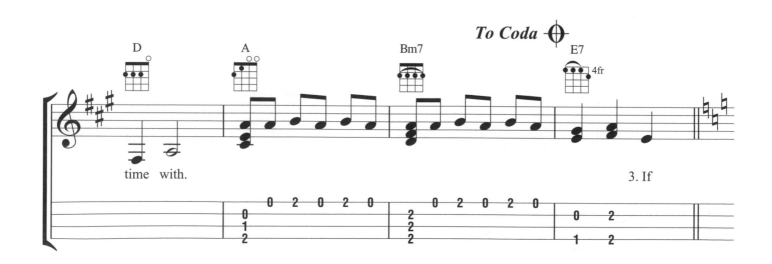

time with.   3. If

Verse

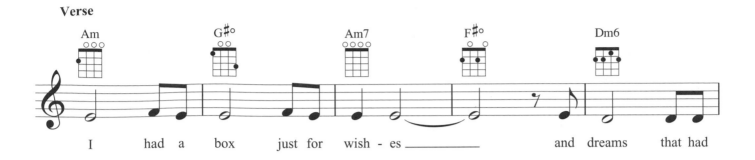

I had a box just for wish - es _____ and dreams that had

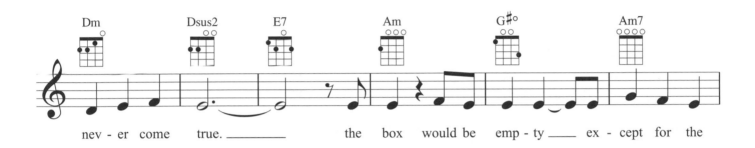

nev - er come true. _____ the box would be emp - ty ___ ex - cept for the

D.S. al Coda

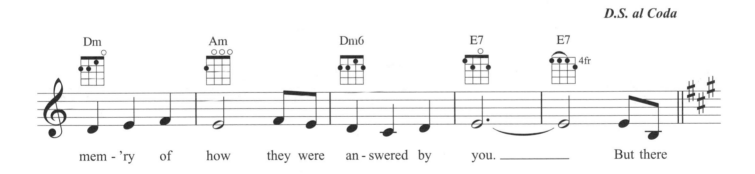

mem - 'ry of how they were an - swered by you. _____ But there

⊕ **Coda**

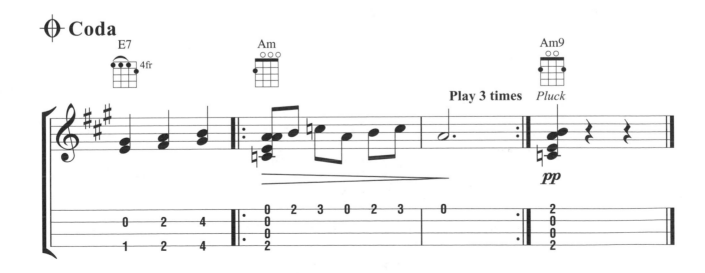

Tiny Bubbles

Words and Music by Leon Pober

Bridge

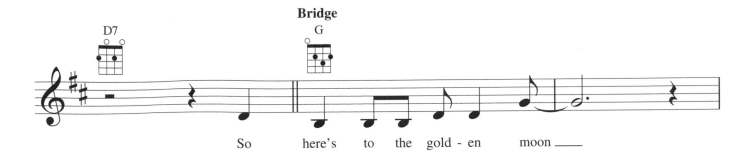

So here's to the gold - en moon ____

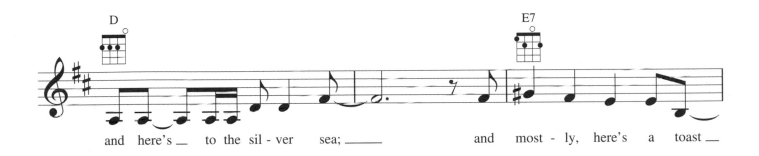

and here's ____ to the sil - ver sea; ____ and most - ly, here's a toast ____

D.S. al Coda

____ to you and me. ____ 2. Ti - ny

Coda

Verse

3. Ti - ny bub - bles ____ in the wine

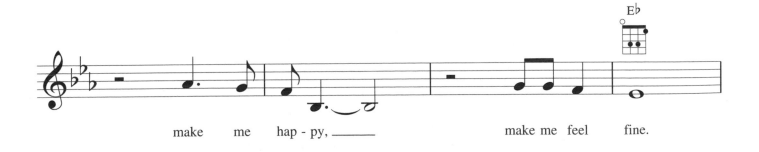

make me hap - py, ____ make me feel fine.

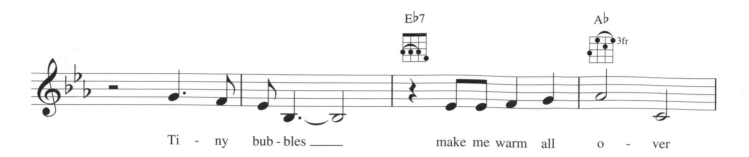

Ti - ny bub - bles _____ make me warm all o - ver

with a feel - in' that I'm gon - na love _____ you till the end _____ of

Outro

time, with a feel - in' that I'm gon - na love _____

_____ you, gon - na love you _____ till the end of

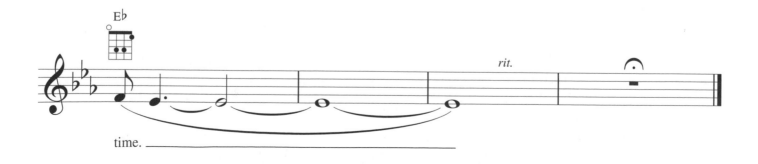

time. _____

26 Miles (Santa Catalina)

Words and Music by Glen Larson and Bruce Belland

trop - i - cal   trees   and   the   salt - y   air, ___   but for
San - ta   Cat - a - li - na   is   a - wait - in'   for   me, ___

me   the   thing   that's   a - wait - in'   there's ___   ro - mance. ___
San - ta   Cat - a - li - na,   the   is - land   of ___   ro - mance. ___

Bridge

___   It   seems   so   dis - tant
___   A   trop - i - cal   heav - en

Twen - ty - six   miles ___   a - way,   rest - in'   in   the   wa - ter   se - rene. ___
out   in   the   o - cean,   cov - ered   with   trees ___   and   girls. ___

___   I'd   work   for   an - y - one,
___   If   I   have   to   swim, _____   I'll

e - ven   the   Na - vy,   who would   float   me   to   my   is - land
do   it   for - ev - er   till   I'm   gaz - in'   on   those   is - land

Verse

G7   N.C.   C   Am   Dm7   G7

dream.   3. Twen - ty - six miles, so near, yet far. ___ I'd
pearls.   5. For - ty kil - o - me - ters in a leak - y old boat, ___

C   Am   Dm7   G7

swim with just some wa - ter wings and my gui - tar. ___ I can
an - y old thing that - 'll stay a - float. ___ When

C   Am   Dm7   G7

leave the wings, but I'll need the gui - tar ___ for ro - mance, ___
we ar - rive we'll all pro - mote ___ ro - mance, ___

2nd time, D.C. al Coda

C   Am   Dm7   G7

___ ro - mance, ___ ro - mance, ___ ro - mance. ___
___ ro - mance, ___ ro - mance, ___ ro - mance. ___

Coda
Outro-Verse

C   Am   Dm7   G7

Twen - ty - six miles a - cross the sea ___

Repeat and fade

C   Am   Dm7   G7

San - ta Cat - a - li - na is a - wait - in' for me. ___

Walkin' After Midnight

Lyrics by Don Hecht
Music by Alan W. Block

First note

Verse

1. I go out walk-in' _____ af-ter mid-night, _____ out in the

moon-light, _____ just _____ like we used to do. I'm al-ways

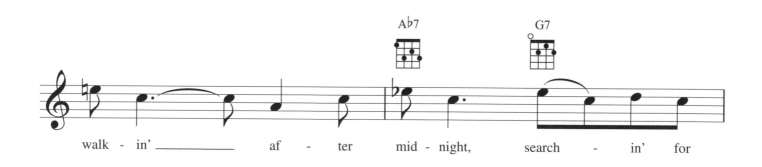

walk-in' _____ af-ter mid-night, search-in' for

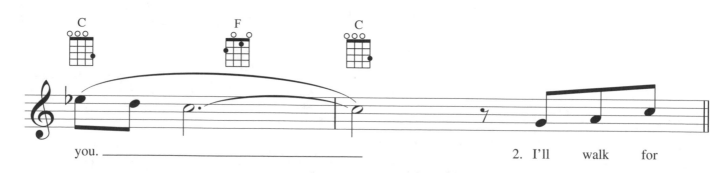

you. _____ 2. I'll walk for

Yellow Submarine

Words and Music by John Lennon and Paul McCartney

We all live in a yel - low sub - ma - rine,
rine.
rine.

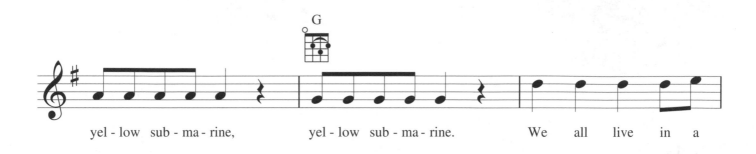

yel - low sub - ma - rine,   yel - low sub - ma - rine.   We all live in a

yel - low sub - ma - rine,   yel - low sub - ma - rine,   yel - low sub - ma - rine. 2. And our friends _

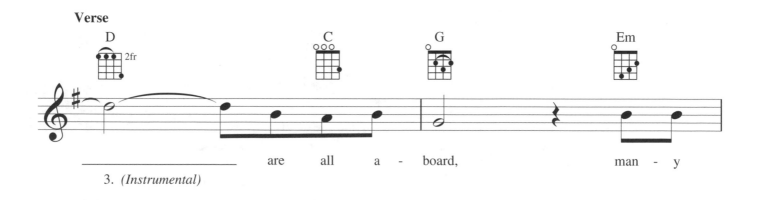

Verse

_____ are all a - board,   man - y

3. *(Instrumental)*

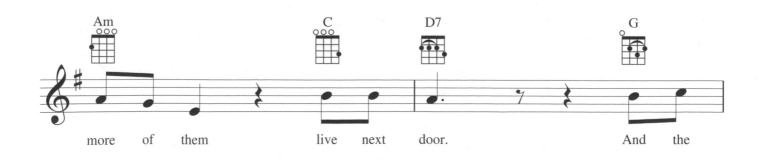

more of them   live next door.   And the

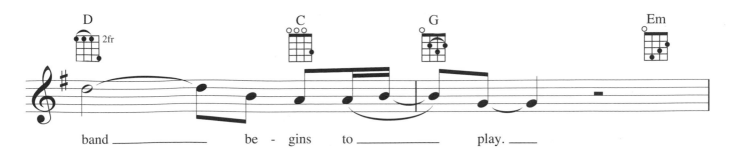

band _____ be - gins to _____ play. ____

D.S. al Coda

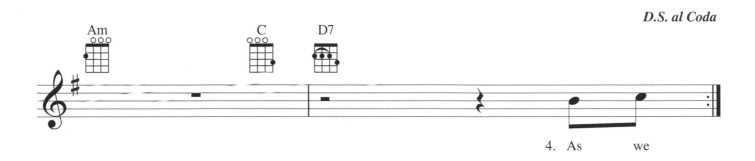

4. As we

Coda

Chorus

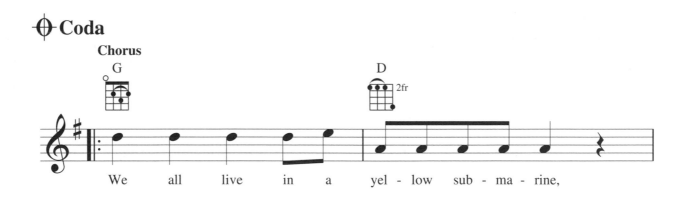

We all live in a yel - low sub - ma - rine,

Repeat and fade

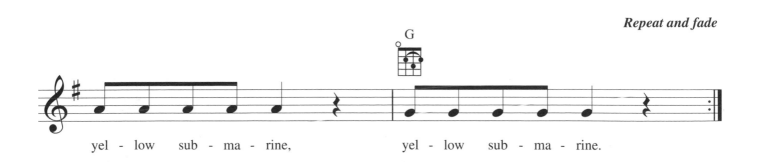

yel - low sub - ma - rine,   yel - low sub - ma - rine.

What the World Needs Now Is Love

Lyrics by Hal David
Music by Burt Bacharach

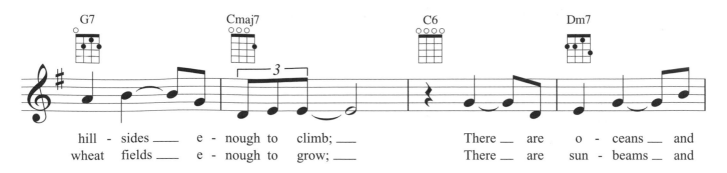

hill - sides ____ e - nough to climb; ____   There __ are o - ceans __ and
wheat fields ____ e - nough to grow; ____   There __ are sun - beams __ and

riv - ers ____ e - nough to cross, ____ e - nough to last, ____   till the end of
moon - beams _ e - nough to shine, ____ oh, lis - ten, Lord, ____   if you want to

Coda

time. ____ What the
know. __ ____ What the

ev - 'ry - one. ____

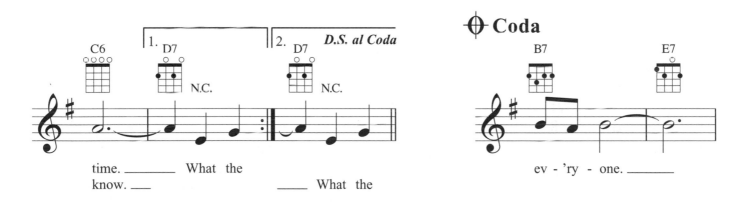

No, not just for some, ____ Oh, but just for

ev - 'ry - one. ____

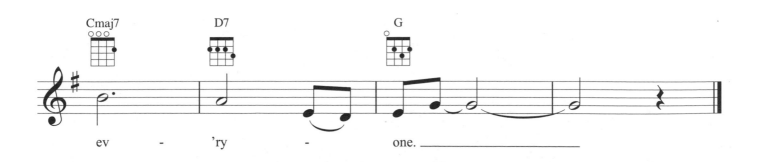

Yellow Bird

Words and Music by Irving Burgie

You Are My Sunshine

Words and Music by Jimmie Davis

First note

Verse

Moderately fast ♩ = 144

1. The oth - er night, dear, _____ as I lay
(2.) love you _____ and make you
(3.) once, dear, _____ you real - ly

sleep - ing, _____ I dreamed I held you _____ in my
hap - py _____ if you will on - ly _____ say the
loved me _____ and no one else could _____ come be -

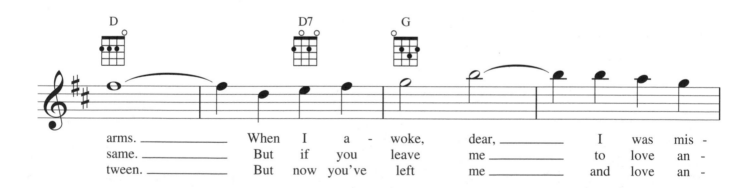

arms. _____ When I a - woke, dear, _____ I was mis -
same. _____ But if you leave me _____ to love an -
tween. _____ But now you've left me _____ and love an -

tak - en _____ and I hung my head and
oth - er, _____ you'll re - gret it all some
oth - er, _____ you have shat - tered all my

Chorus

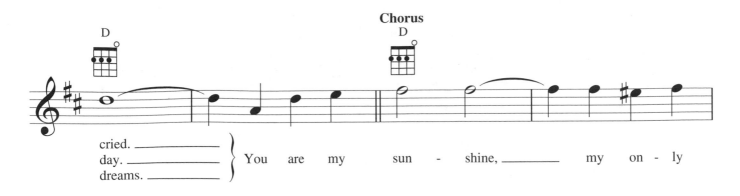

cried. _____
day. _____ } You are my sun - shine, _____ my on - ly
dreams. _____

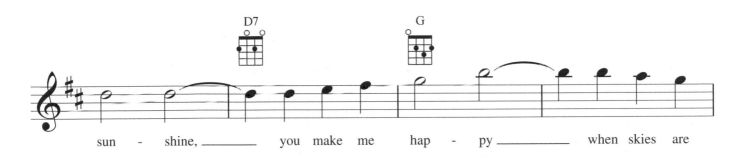

sun - shine, _____ you make me hap - py _____ when skies are

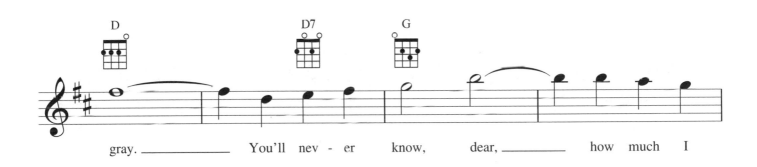

gray. _____ You'll nev - er know, dear, _____ how much I

love you. _____ Please don't take my sun - shine a -

1., 2.   3.

way. _____
{ 2. I'll al - ways
{ 3. You told me _____

Chord and Scale Charts

Here are some of the most commonly played ukulele chords for reference.

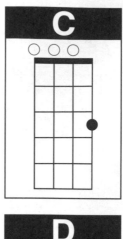
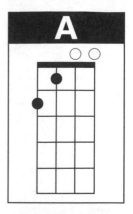
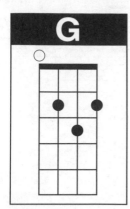
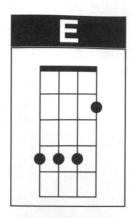

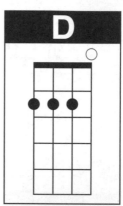
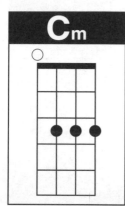
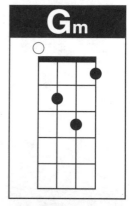
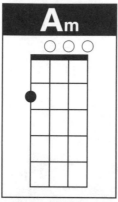

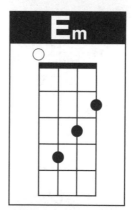
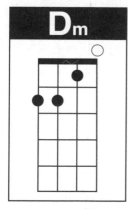
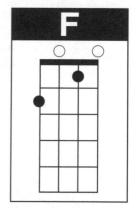
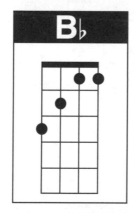

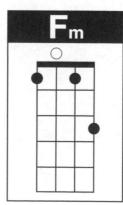
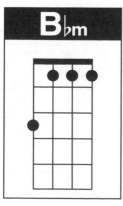
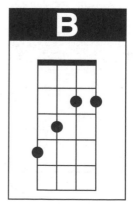
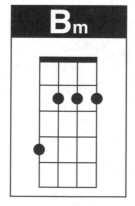

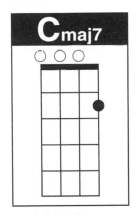

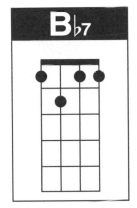

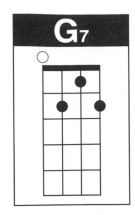

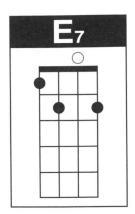

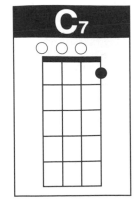

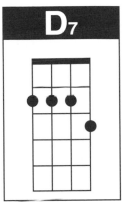

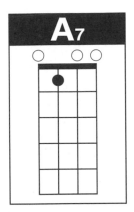

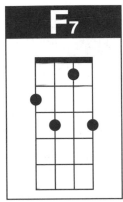

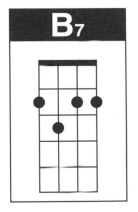

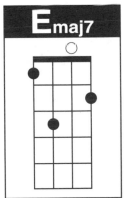

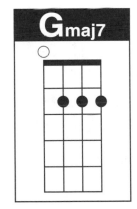

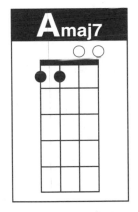

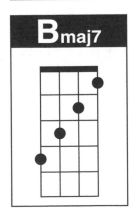

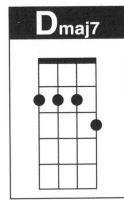

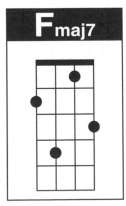

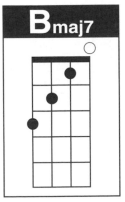

The Major Scale

The major scale is the backbone of Western music. Almost all pop melodies and chords can be derived from it, and it's by far the most important scale to know how to play. Shown here are all 12 major scales in open position, or as close to open position as possible. Note that the root note will not always be the lowest note of the scale; each root note is shown as an open circle on the diagrams so you can keep your place.

Playing scales this way, from the lowest note to the highest note possible in one position, is an excellent way to familiarize yourself with the instrument. Rather than just moving the same scale shape up and down the neck to play in different keys, this method will allow to you play most of the melodies in this book in the same position, as the range of most will generally fall within the area of the first four frets or so. (Some melodies may need to be transposed down an octave from their written range.) A moveable form is provided as well, which will allow you to play any major scale by sliding up or down the neck. Note that it resembles the C major scale, except that the open strings have been replaced with fretted notes.

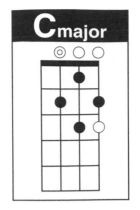

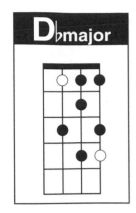

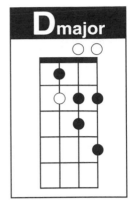

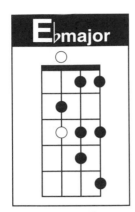

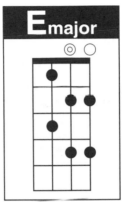

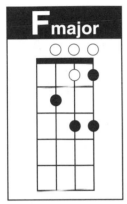

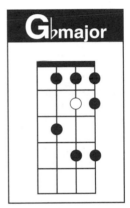

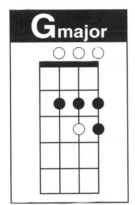

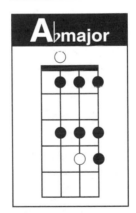

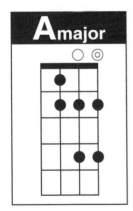

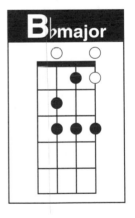

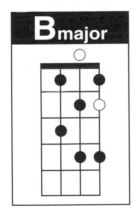

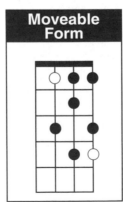

Basic Chord Harmony

This section is intended to provide a basic knowledge of chords, how to build them, and how to use them. Some of you may already know this; if so, go catch a matinee or something. If not, read on and learn how to impress your friends who don't know.

Triads

A chord is simply a collection of notes deliberately arranged in a harmonious (or sometimes non-harmonious) fashion. The most common type of chord is called a triad. The name triad is telling you the number of notes in the chord: three. Triads can be one of four different qualities: major, minor, augmented, or diminished. The accompanying figure shows the C Major triad.

The words root, third, and fifth below the notes on the staff indicate how each note functions within the chord. A root note is the foundation of the chord and the note after which the chord will be named.

The word triad is often used interchangeably with the word chord. If you hear someone say, "Play a C chord," that's the same as saying play a C triad.

Intervals

The other two notes in our C triad (the 3rd and the 5th) are responsible for the quality of the chord. The notes C and E are an *interval* (or distance) of a major 3rd apart. Intervals are comprised of two components: a number and a quality.

The number part is easy. You can determine that C to E is a 3rd by simply counting through the musical alphabet. Starting from C: C is one, D is two, and E is three. (The word root is often used interchangeably with the number 1. For all practical purposes, they mean the same thing.) From C to G is a 5th, and you can confirm this by again counting up from C: C(1)-D(2)-E(3)-F(4)-G(5).

Determining the quality of an interval isn't quite as easy and will require a bit of memorization, but it's very logical. The accompanying figure shows all 12 notes in the chromatic scale and their intervals measured from a C root note.

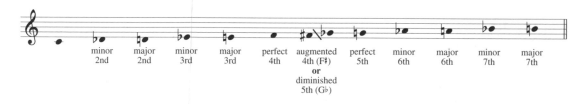

You can see a few formulas here at work. The first thing you should notice is that a minor interval is always one half step smaller than a major interval. C to E is a major 3rd, whereas C to E♭ is a minor 3rd. C to A is a major 6th, whereas C to A♭ is a minor 6th, and so on.

The next thing you should notice is how 4ths and 5ths work. You can see that an augmented interval is always one half step greater than a perfect one, and a diminished interval is always one half step smaller.

Any triad of one of the four qualities will contain a root, 3rd, and 5th. Other types of triads you may encounter include 6 chords, sus4 chords, and sus2 chords. Theses chords are the product of (in the case of sus4 and sus2 chords) replacing the 3rd with another note or (in the case of 6 chords) replacing the 5th (or sometimes adding to it) with another note.

The accompanying figure shows several different qualities of triads which will allow you to examine these intervals at work and note how they affect the names of these chords.

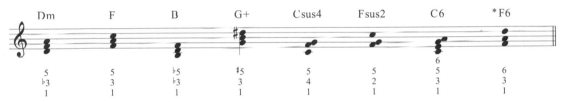

The symbol ° stands for diminished, while the symbol + stands for augmented.
* Note that the 5th tone may or may not be present in a 6 chord.

7th Chords

Beyond the triad, you encounter many more chords, most commonly 7th chords. These chords will not only contain the root, 3rd, and 5th, but also the 7th. The accompanying figure shows a few common 7th chords. (Note that the 7th interval may be major or minor independent of the 3rd, thus affecting the name of the chord.)

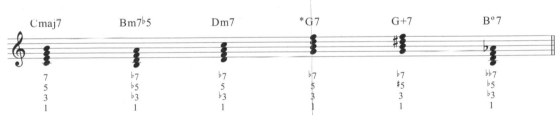

* Note that the G7 chord contains a major 3rd and a minor 7th. This type of chord is referred to as a *dominant 7th*.

Extensions

Finally, beyond 7th chords, you have extensions. The concept of extensions is a bit complicated and will only be touched upon here, as it requires more extensive study than is possible within the scope of this book.

Basically, extended chords continue the process of stacking notes onto a triad that we began with the 7th chord. Instead of only adding the 7th to the chord, however, in a 9th chord you'll add the 7th and the 9th to your triad. In an 11th chord, you'll add the 7th, 9th, and 11th to our triad, and so on.

Now, here's the catch: not all the notes need to be present in an extended chord. The general rule is, if the 7th is present, then notes other than the root, 3rd, and 5th are extensions and therefore numbered an octave higher (9, 11, 13). Since you're only capable of playing four notes at a time on the ukulele, you must decide which notes are important and which notes you can omit.

Generally speaking, you'll want to include the root, 3rd, 7th, and the extension. The C13 chord shown here demonstrates this concept:

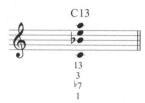

Note that there is no 5th (G) present in this chord, but the presence of the 7th (B♭) tells you that this chord is called C13, rather than some kind of C6 chord.

Inversions

Because the ukulele only has four strings, chords will often be voiced in *inversion*. A chord is inverted when a note other than the root is in the bass. In a triad, which contains three different notes, there are three basic possibilities for the vertical organization of the notes: root position, first inversion, and second inversion. Chords in root position contain the root of the chord in the bass; in other words, they are not inversions. A first inversion chord, however, contains the 3rd in the bass, while a second inversion chord contains the 5th in the bass. This is demonstrated in the accompanying figure.

In a seventh chord or an extended chord, which contains four different notes, you have another inversion possibility. In addition to the first and second inversions, you can also have a third inversion, which places the 7th of the chord in the bass.

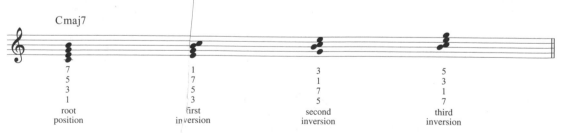

Again, this section is intended to be a basic tutorial on the concept of chord construction and chord theory. If you're interested in furthering your knowledge on this subject, I suggest you take a look at some of the many books dedicated to chord construction and theory, such as *Music Theory For Dummies* (Wiley) by Michael Pilhofer and Holly Day.